ROBOTIC GOLF

How a High-Handicap Golfer Can Become a
Single-Digit Golfer by a Guy Who Did It

LARRY CARPENTER

Clovercroft Publishing

Robotic Golf

© 2022 by Larry Carpenter

Published by Clovercroft Publishing, Franklin, Tennessee

Edited by David Brown

Photographs by Craig Carpenter

Cover and Interior Design by Suzanne Lawing

Printed in the United States of America

978-1-954437-28-9

This book is dedicated to Madison Whittemore, Brian Jorgenson, and the loyal and dedicated staff at the Nashville Golf and Athletic Club. They have built a first-class golf facility that is always a pleasure to play. How they have put up with me as a member since 1994 is a mystery to me!

Acknowledgment

Several people have inspired me in my pursuit of improvement in golf and in the writing of this book. The name of the first person, unfortunately, remains nameless. After seriously taking up the game in my thirties, I struggled to teach myself how to play. A wicked slice drove me to take my first lesson. I took one lesson from a young pro at Nashboro Village Golf Club. I wish I remembered his name, but I don't. After watching me hit one banana ball after another, he confidently said, "We can fix that." And he did. He told me to move my hands around and strengthen my grip. I didn't know that was legal! It was a simple fix. But it set me on the path to realize that we can make mechanical changes that improve our game.

My second influential lesson came from Brian Jorgenson, who now serves as the Pro Emeritus at Nashville Golf and Athletic Club. From Brian, I learned that golf should be fun. He taught me to hit the ball with focus and confidence.

My third influential lesson came from Scott Pierce, who, at the time, was the head pro at Forrest Crossing Golf Club. I played a fund-raising tournament at the course. Afterwards, they had a silent auction. Just to get things started, I wrote down a low-ball bid for two lessons from Scott. I guess no one else needed lessons, so my bid held up. I got two lessons from Scott at way below his regular fee. Scott taught me that golf instruction can never be "one size fits all." Every golfer is different. He adapted his teaching method to the skill level and abilities of the golfer. He didn't expect me to be able to hit the ball the way he hit it. That started me on the road to what became "robotic golf."

A special thanks goes to Bob Vocker. Bob has taught people to play golf for over fifty years. Most recently, Bob served as the Director of Golf at the Woodbridge Golf & Country Club. It's no secret that some of my techniques are at odds with what the pros teach. But Bob made sure that I didn't get too far out there! A large part of "robotic golf" is sticking with the basics of good golf technique. Bob made sure the basics were covered and the techniques I espoused were sound.

I would also like to thank my editor, David Brown. And I want to thank the best book designer in the world, Suzanne Lawing, for the wonderful cover and interior layout design. Finally, I would like to give my son, Craig, a special thanks for taking the photos used in the book.

Contents

INTRODUCTION

For years and years, amateur golfers have been going to see pros to learn how to improve their game. If there were some major technical difficulties in their game, the amateurs could come away from the lessons with an improved game. But for most of us, we might see an improvement or two under the watchful eye of the pro, but when we returned back to the course, our bad golf game simply returned. Even if we remembered the technical changes, we simply could not hit the ball on the sweet spot time after time like the pro.

There is a very simple explanation as to why this is the case. The golf pro has good hand-eye coordination, and you don't. Or at least, if you're reading this book, you most likely don't. If you are blessed with good hand-eye coordination and you simply don't have good technique, go see the pro. You have a lot in common. You just need to learn what they know.

But if you struggle to transfer the knowledge imparted to you by the pro, or the golf instructional book or video, does this mean that the instructor is a bad instructor? Not at all. It just means that the instructor is providing information to you on how they play their best golf. But playing their best golf is based on playing with their level of athleticism, overall body coordination, timing, and hand-eye coordination. The bottom line is that, if you don't share those same skills with them, the instruction that they provide you most likely won't work for you.

Here's an illustration of what I am talking about. In his book *Best Seat in the House*, Jack Nicklaus's son Jackie tells a story about what happened early in his professional career. He went to see a sports psychologist, Bob Rotella. The psychologist gave him a homework assignment. He was to ask his father a series of questions. Here's what Jackie said in the book:

"I asked Dad the questions, but he never answered them. Dad is rather old school and was reluctant to embrace the benefits of working with a sports psychologist. He wasn't convinced that Bob could help me. 'If I have to concentrate, I just do it,' Dad said."

Later, Jackie writes:

> "What I learned in that moment is that, like many elite athletes, Dad couldn't explain to me what he did that made him special. We all know how few great players actually become great coaches because often, what they do, how they think, isn't transferable knowledge."

And that's what I'm talking about. Many of the things that Jack Nicklaus did were due to his innate talent. When asked to explain how he did what he did, he drew a blank. So, you can imagine what happened when a publisher said to him, "Okay

---

Jack Nicklaus II, *Best Seat in the House: 18 Golden Lessons from a Father to His Son* (Nashville, Tennessee: Thomas Nelson, 2021)

Jack, we're going to write a book to tell everybody else how you do what you do." It's just not going to happen.

If you are reading this book, you are never going to be able to hit the ball like Jack Nicklaus. For the rest of us, it simply boils down to the fact that we are not blessed with great hand-eye coordination like the pure ball strikers that you see on the television each weekend. Does this mean that we are doomed to forever be relegated to the land of the high handicap? For years, I thought that was the case. But when I realized what the basic problem was, I was able to develop an alternative technique that helped me improve my game. Using this technique, I was able to take my handicap from the high twenties down to single digits. Although I would be hard-pressed to play to this level today, when I first refined my technique, I was able to lower my handicap to an eight.

So, how does a self-admitted bad golfer lower his handicap to single digits? Well, that's what this book is all about. In this

See, I really was able to get my golf handicap down to single digits.
It took a while, but the techniques in this book can work.

book, I will share with you the techniques that I adopted to compensate for not having the incredible hand-eye coordination that single-digit golfers normally possess. But let me warn you. Much of what I say in this book would be met by a rousing round of laughter from the average club professional. Why? Because I'm going to tell you things which they will tell you are dead wrong.

But here's the thing. Virtually every professional is going to tell you to not be very mechanical. Later in the book, we'll get into why they tell you this. But the bottom line is that an athlete with good hand-eye coordination can easily swing the club that is four feet long and make contact with a one-inch object in the center of their clubface. But I can't do that. If you've gotten this far in the book, you are probably in the same boat.

Therefore, if you don't have the same level of hand-eye coordination and athletic ability that the pros have, you have to compensate. When they say, "Don't be mechanical, play by feel," you simply have to realize that if you try to hit the ball by feel, you're going to whiff it. And you're going to be continually frustrated by your high handicap. Hence, the technique that I developed. This technique is based upon mechanical principles that enable the less blessed golfer to compensate for their lack of hand-eye coordination and stand a much better chance of making solid contact with the ball every swing.

There's one other way in which this book will differ from your average golf instructional book. In the famous instructional books by Ben Hogan, Jack Nicklaus, and other really good golfers, they provide instruction on virtually all elements of the golf game. So, in their chapter on getting out of the bunker, they will tell you what stance to assume, how to open the clubface, and so forth. But the purpose of this book is to provide you with the technique that helps you make solid contact with the ball. If there is a technique that is common for both the high-handicap golfer and the professional, such as how to assume an open stance, we are not going to spend a lot of time on it. Go ahead and buy Jack Nicklaus's excellent instructional book. Use his techniques to become the best golfer you can. But remember, his suggestions only become beneficial if you are making solid contact with the ball. And that's where this book comes in.

If, after reading the book, you are tempted to say, "But he didn't talk about so and so," that's because there's really nothing that I can add to what the best professionals advise on that topic. This book is simply to be used as a supplement to those books written by the pros. In other words, this book is simply designed to give you techniques to compensate for your lack of hand-eye coordination, and to make solid contact with the ball, so that you can then benefit from their knowledge.

Good luck, and I hope that you find the techniques in this book to be helpful.

THE SECRET
TO THE GAME

The secret to golf is a repeating swing. A golf swing doesn't have to be a thing of beauty. Watch the swings of Lee Trevino, Jim Furyk, and Matthew Wolff. None of these three golfers have what is considered to be a classic swing. But how can that be? How can they be among the best golfers around without executing their skills with the generally accepted method of doing so? The answer is that, despite what their club does in the backswing and downswing, they return the club to the ball with the same recurring, predictable swing every time.

Basically, you want your club to return to the back of the ball with two essential requirements. First, the clubface should be totally neutral when it strikes the ball (except in the case of a specialty shot, such as a draw or fade). A neutral clubface at contact is key to hitting the ball straight. Secondly, you want to make contact with the ball in the center of the clubface. The more the ball deviates from making contact in the center of the clubface, or "sweet spot," the more power will be robbed from your swing. As long as those two requirements are met at the conclusion of your backswing and downswing, it doesn't really matter what your club does when it goes backward and when it goes forward.

However, that being said, you don't want to do something different every time. Again, watch Jim Furyk's swing. Despite the loop and everything that he does in his swing, he still does the same thing every time. This is what we mean by a repeating swing. And that repeating swing is the key to making good contact with the ball. You want to make a swing that brings your clubface to the back of the ball with those two requirements met each and every time you swing.

Long after I knew this to be true, I still struggled to master a repeating swing. Until, one day, I saw a video showing the best example of a repeating swing. That video was of Iron Byron. If you don't know, Iron Byron is the robot that is used by equipment manufacturers and the regulatory bodies of golf to measure balls and clubs in a consistent manner. Since Iron Byron swings at exactly the same speed, angle, swing plane,

*The Iron Byron machine makes the same
consistent contact with the ball every time.*

etc. each time, it is the best way to measure how clubs and balls perform under exactly the same circumstances.

Byron Nelson is one of the greatest golfers of all time. He still holds the record for winning the most consecutive professional golf tournaments. He is largely credited as the "Father of the Modern Golf Swing." Stories are told about how, after hitting a bucket of balls, his caddie only had to walk to a small circle to retrieve all of the balls.

In 1963, golf manufacturer True Temper commissioned engineer George Manning to design a robotic machine that would hit a golf ball the same way every time. His first step was to review footage of dozens of professional golfers to find the "perfect" swing. After his review was completed, he

Byron Nelson- The man with the perfect swing.

decided that the golfer with the most perfect swing was Byron Nelson. Therefore, he named his machine Iron Byron.

For years, the United States Golf Association (USGA) has used Iron Byron for all its testing of clubs and balls. The story is told that the USGA has to change out the turf in their testing area every two years. Since Iron Byron hits the ball so consistently, it eventually damages the turf where the thousands of balls land.

Once I knew that I had to be like Iron Byron and make contact with the back of the ball in a predictable consistent manner, I could go to work. Having taken numerous lessons, I had heard the pros say the same thing each time. "Don't get too mechanical in your swing. You want to learn to play with feel." Well, I tried the feel approach. I didn't exactly whiff the ball. I do have a decent level of hand-eye coordination. But I sure didn't hit the ball anywhere near the sweet spot every time.

Before we go any further, let's define our terms. A golfer who plays by feel avoids thinking too much about the way that they swing the club (the mechanics of the swing). They simply take a nice fluid swing. While they are conscious of where the ball is, they aren't "ball bound." Pros tell you to be more focused on the target, not the ball. The story is told that Ben Hogan, playing a new course, asked the caddie where to aim his shot. The caddie told him to aim toward a group of trees. Ben Hogan asked, "Which tree?" Pros and good golfers feel like a concentrated focus on the ball prevents the golfer from focusing on where they want to hit the ball. I once had a pro who told me to remove everything from my mind, swing the club back, and swing the club through. He told me not to try to hit the ball. Just swing through where I "felt" the ball was and let the ball get in the way of the club.

In contrast, a mechanical golfer feels like they have to have every piece of a golf swing predetermined and locked in place. Ask a mechanical golfer where his right elbow needs to be in his swing, and he can immediately answer the question. Ask a feel golfer and you'll get an answer like, "Gee, I don't know. I never thought about it." A mechanical golfer doesn't just swing the club back as far as it feels right to hit the ball a certain distance. Instead, they use techniques like imagining their body as the face of a clock. They know that to hit their lob wedge thirty yards, they need to pull their arms back to "eight o'clock."

Mechanical golfers tend to have lots of swing thoughts. If they are lucky, they only think about one or two in their actual swing. But there aren't many lucky, bad golfers! Most crowd their minds with too many thoughts, and then wonder why they lost their focus on making solid contact with the back of the ball.

Stories are told about how feel golfers wrecked their game by trying to become more mechanical. Perhaps the most common example was Seve Ballesteros. Seve was one of the foremost feel golfers. He started out with just one club. So, he had to make that one club be able to hit every shot, from a drive to a putt. He determined how to hit each shot by using his intuition, creativity, and feel. Off the tee, he didn't always drill his drive down the middle of the fairway. He won the 1979 Open by hitting his approach shot on hole number sixteen from the parking lot! But he was a wizard around the green. Later in his career, though, he began to doubt his feel and tried to overanalyze his golf swing. This led to a more mechanical swing. Golf instructors will tell you that this is the best example of why you should play by feel and avoid becoming too mechanical in your swing.

I understand why pros don't want to get too mechanical. Frankly, it crowds the brain. Thinking about so many things causes a good golfer to become so distracted that they don't execute their smooth swing, which just happens to make solid contact with the ball. The analogy used most often by the instructors is comparing the golf swing to the free throw shooter. They ask you how you analyze how far to shoot a basketball. Or, for that matter, how do you analyze how much thrust to use when throwing a ball of paper toward the trash can? They point out that if a basketball player gets too mechanical about their free throw, they will crowd their brain and miss the shot more often than they make it. So, they reason, you should hit a golf ball like you shoot a free throw. Maybe think about one mechanical thought or two (knees bent, hands held high, etc.) BEFORE you shoot the free throw. But, once you are ready to take the shot, let your mind go blank and just aim for the target.

Simple enough. Why doesn't that work for the uncoordinated golfer? Because there's not a sweet spot in the palm of your hand! You don't have to make solid contact with a basketball before you hit it. But you do have to hit the golf ball in the sweet spot. I can shoot a basketball using just feel. But I can't make solid contact in the sweet spot of my golf club every time simply by feel. I need some mechanical help.

Let me leave you with one final thought on feel versus mechanical. Let's focus on the folks with the best coordination in the game, the golf professionals. Listen to the announcers. They will say that a certain golfer is one of the best "ball strikers" in the business. Or the winning pro will say that he or she was "striking the ball well that day." What does a good ball striker do? Hit the ball right in the sweet spot! So, let's say that 10 percent of the pros get the reputation for being a great ball striker. What does that mean? It means that 90 percent of the greatest golfers in the world aren't hitting the ball consistently in the sweet spot! Think about that for a second. That doesn't bode well for the rest of us. So, let the good golfers focus on hitting the ball by feel. The rest of us are going to learn how to hit the ball with good mechanics!

What is the purpose of a mechanical, robotic swing? You may have heard the term "problem/solution." From the perspective of my day job as a book publisher, I can tell you that the best self-help books have a problem/solution orientation. There must be a problem that the book is addressing. And the book must have a solid, workable solution to the problem. The problem for the high handicap golfer is simple. We are struggling just to make good solid contact with the ball. Our drives might not go three hundred yards. But, if we are able to consistently hit our drives two hundred yards down the middle of the fairway, or at least not in trouble, we would be happy.

To begin to understand the secrets of how a bad golfer becomes a good golfer, we first need to understand what it is that makes us bad. In other words, what is it that those good amateur golfers and professionals can do that we cannot? As discussed earlier, it's called hand-eye coordination.

There are many things that you can do like a pro. You can wear the same clothes that they wear. You can use the same golf ball. You can use the same clubs. You can play the same courses. You can use many of the same techniques that they use. But here's the bad news. They have good hand-eye coordination and you don't. But what exactly is this elusive hand-eye coordination?

Here is the technical definition. **Hand-eye coordination, or eye-hand coordination**, is the ability to do activities that require the simultaneous use of our **hands** and **eyes**, like an activity that uses the information our **eyes** perceive (visual spatial perception) to guide our **hands** to carry out a movement.

Hand-eye coordination is relatively easy to measure. If you have a small spot on the wall, stand approximately three feet away. Now, reach out and place your index finger squarely on the spot. Someone with good hand-eye coordination will hit the spot virtually every time. But those of us who are not blessed with the greatest hand-eye coordination find that much more difficult to do. Sure, we're going to hit the spot every once in a while. Call that dumb luck. We might be half an inch off. We might be an inch off. But we struggle to be able to signal to our finger exactly where our brain tells us the spot resides.

In sports, it becomes more obvious, especially if it's a sport that involves a process that takes place some distance from the body. People with not the greatest hand-eye coordination probably make fine wrestlers. They might make a decent offensive lineman. But they would struggle to hit a fastball with the bat that has a contact point about two feet away from the end of their hands. Forget that career as a wide receiver. Where your eyes tell you that football is spiraling into is not where your hands generally are placed to catch it.

In some games where the process takes place away from your body, you can compensate. For example, people with less than stellar hand-eye coordination can make decent tennis players. Why? Because they have a much bigger sweet spot on an oversized tennis racket, and they are hitting an object that is about three times the size of a golf ball. Don't get me wrong. Is someone who has poor hand-eye coordination ever going to win at Wimbledon? Of course not. Tennis professionals have incredible hand-eye coordination and can control their shots by hitting them at the exact point on the racket that they need to hit them. But because of the wider sweet spot on the tennis racket and the larger size of the tennis ball, the negative effect of a less than stellar hand-eye coordination is not as noticeable as it is in golf.

Think about it. In golf, you are trying to hit a small object on the sweet spot that is only about an inch or less wide, using an object that extends out three to four feet from your arm, which is extended out by two feet or more from your body. It's no surprise that the average golfer lives a life of frustration as they never can hit the golf ball with the consistency of the good amateurs and the pros.

But the good news is that there are techniques that you can use to compensate for this lack of hand-eye coordination. If you aren't naturally able to return a club in the downswing to the point that your eye has identified that you need it to be to make solid contact with the ball, then you need some mechanical techniques to be able to accomplish this. That's what this book is all about.

If it is so obvious what we need to do this, why don't pros incorporate this into their teaching? Some do. The ones who have figured out that the average Joe simply does not have the level of athleticism and hand-eye coordination that they do have learned some of these techniques. But the sad fact of the matter, as you probably learned if you went to a pro for a lesson, is that the vast majority of pros do not teach these techniques.

Why? Well first, let me assure you that it is not that they are not trying to help you. The average pro really wants to help you improve your golf game. Why wouldn't they? A happy, successful student is going to recommend that golf pro to other frustrated golfers. That translates to increased money and a good livelihood.

So, what's the problem? The problem is that the average pro has a set of techniques and skills that they simply assume that everyone else has. If you have good hand-eye coordination, and your finger hits the spot every time, it's hard for you to imagine people who don't share a similar level of skill. If you are able to casually swing the club, or even swing it at unimaginable speeds and still make solid contact with the ball, you have a difficult time taking your mind out of that mindset and placing it into a place where that is simply impossible to do.

I know it's a cliché, but the old adage about walking a mile in someone else's shoes is good solid advice. But here's the flaw in that adage. It requires you to get into the mind and body of that other person. How can a pro who has never experienced a severe lack of hand-eye coordination think and act like someone who has? It's very difficult to do.

Secondly, the techniques that someone with poor hand-eye coordination has to use are diametrically opposed to the techniques taught by the pro to create the best golf swings. One of the most common statements that you will hear from the pros, either in the lesson or in the golf instructional books is, "Do not get too mechanical." You'll also hear things like, "Don't try to hit the ball. Just swing the club and let the ball get in the way." You'll hear the pros caution against "becoming too ball-bound."

Here are a couple of examples that illustrate the way the pros think. First, let's go back to the story about Ben Hogan. Remember the one about how his caddie told him to aim at the cluster of trees and he asked, "Which tree?" This illustrates two things. First, it illustrates Ben Hogan's ability to hit the ball where he wanted to! But for our purposes, it illustrates that the pros are generally teaching you to look at your target, and not your ball. It's easy for them to suggest that you focus on your target and not your ball because they have no problem making solid contact with the ball. They don't have to focus all of their attention on the ball to simply make contact with it like us high-handicap golfers have to do.

Here's another example. In putting, have you ever had a pro tell you not to focus your attention on the ball, but rather focus on the direction you're putting or the speed with which you are putting? Or even more illustrative, have you ever had a pro suggest that you place your focus on the hole itself, rather than on the ball. Sure, I tried it once or twice. But after almost whiffing the putt, I realized that these pros were working from a frame of reference and talent which I simply did not have.

Why is it that even given the pro's greater hand-eye coordination that they are so negative about playing golf in a mechanical fashion? Why is it that they place so much emphasis on feel? Or put more simply, why can they not see that the rest of us simply are not capable of playing golf by feel like they are. After all, instructors in other sports are able to see and adapt to the limitations of their less gifted students. For example, a pee wee football coach doesn't expect their eight-year-olds to play like a Pittsburgh Steeler. They adapt their technique to the skill level of the player. Why can't a golf pro do the same?

The major reason is that the pee wee football coach KNOWS that his kids can't do what an older football player can do. But a golf pro looks at a golfer who, on the surface, appears very similar to them and assumes that they should be able to do what they do. And the mechanical technique that the high-handicap golfer needs to achieve the goal of solid contact with the ball is the antithesis of the technique they know helps them to make solid contact with the ball. Let's go back to the issue with being a mechanical golfer.

Remember, the pro believes that when golfers get too mechanical, they tend to overanalyze things. Analyzing your golf game is not a bad idea. But not right in the middle of your shot. Some pros, such as Bryson DeChambeau, are known for their intense analysis of every aspect of the game. Even the most feel-oriented golfer still uses techniques such as shot tracking equipment, launch monitors, video recordings, and other techniques to analyze their game. That's not what we're talking about.

The negative that we are talking about is getting over your ball and compiling a list of all the factors that can affect your shot. What is the distance to the cup? Which direction will be ball run if I miraculously get it on the green? Am I hitting the ball too close to the bunker on the side? Is my shot uphill or downhill? Is the ball above or below my feet? Which direction is the wind blowing? Should I choke down on this club? How embarrassed will I be if I duff this shot?

If the golfer allows all of these thoughts to be running through their brain during their shot, their chances of hitting a good shot are vastly diminished. And the pro knows that. So, their advice is to weigh all of those questions before you set up over the ball. Once you have answered the questions, selected the best club, and set up for the shot, take your swing with a high degree of confidence that you're going to hit a great shot. And swing with a free-flowing sense of feel.

Here's another way to understand why the pro is so against playing golf in a mechanical fashion. Even beyond the analysis of the shot and the situation, when the golfer begins to focus on the shot, they tend to dredge up every mechanical maneuver that they've ever learned. Do I initiate the swing with some sort of pre-shot cue, such as kicking the knee forward? How low and slow do I start out the club head? How far out do I take my arc? How far back do I swing the club? Is my swing on plane? How do I keep my elbow close to my side? How do I keep my arms straight? What is the position of my wrists at the top? When do I initiate my downswing? What are my feet doing during all of this? Have I braced against the inside of my back foot? How do I hold the lag in my downswing? Am I approaching the ball from outside in or inside out? Should I curl my wrists over in an effort to create a natural draw on the ball? Where do I finish my follow-through?

Sound familiar? These are just some of the hundreds of swing thoughts that you could and do have when you are taking your golf swing. A golf pro would argue that the reason you are having so many swing thoughts is that you are being too mechanical in your swing. If you simply set up over the ball, think of one, or at most, two swing thoughts during the swing, and swing with that free-flowing smooth feel-oriented swing, you would perform much better.

So now you see the problem. The golf pro wants you to banish the mechanical thoughts related to the circumstances of the shot and related to the mechanics of the golf swing itself and take a nice undiluted free-flowing, feel-oriented swing. But if us guys with poor hand-eye coordination follow that advice, the ball contacts the face of the club anywhere but in the sweet spot (and sometimes doesn't even do that)! And we watch as our ball goes everywhere, except where it's supposed to go.

That's why high-handicap golfers need to learn a technique where they are able to set up for the shot in a position where, if they make solid contact with the ball, it's going to end up in the general vicinity where they want it to be. In other words, forget about hitting toward a specific tree or other target. Find that target while you're still standing behind the ball. Use a targeted aiming device in front of your ball, such as a discolored piece of grass to ensure that a shot hit with the clubface in the correct position is going to go in the direction that you want it to go. Factor in your natural tendency to draw or fade the shot. It is said that Moe Norman, who is generally considered to have the most consistent swing in golf, always hit the ball straight. Here's a newsflash. You're not Moe Norman!

Factor your natural tendency into the shot. Next, factor in the outside factors, such as the direction of the wind, the lie of the ball, etc. and set up for the shot. At this point, if you can make a swing that makes solid contact with the ball, you're going to be in great shape. All you need to know are a few simple techniques that will enable you to make solid contact with the ball and, most importantly, give you the confidence that you know that you're going to make solid contact with the ball. That, in essence, is the goal of this book.

THE REPEATING
SWING

The first thing to understand in learning these new techniques is the importance of a repeating swing. Many high-handicap golfers think that their swing has to look like Adam Scott or Steve Stricker every time. These are golfers who are blessed with the most fundamentally sound swings. Golf announcers ooh and ahh when they watch those golfers' swings in slow motion. Your odds of swinging with this level of perfection are slim. But the good news is that a perfect swing is not necessary in order to play good golf. Because for every Adam Scott or Steve Stricker, there's a Lee Trevino, Matthew Wolff, or Jim Furyk.

The stories are told about how natural golfers such as Matthew Wolff or Jim Furyk were told by their early coaches to change the way they hit the ball. Thankfully, neither one of these pros did so. Why? Because they didn't think they needed to. They were able to do exactly what you need to be able to do in order to hit a good golf shot. That is to have a reliable repeating swing.

Jim Furyk famously has a large figure eight in his swing. But to understand why Jim Furyk hits the ball so well is to understand that, despite what his club or clubface does during his backswing and downswing, Jim Furyk almost always repeats the same swing. He brings the clubface down to make solid contact with the golf ball in the same way virtually every time. Remember, you don't hit the ball during your backswing. Your backswing is simply taking the club back so that all of those laws that Isaac Newton came up with can kick in. Gravity. Inertia. Centrifugal force. And all the rest. The backswing simply pulls the rubber band of the slingshot back so that it can propel the pebble out as fast as possible.

Now, don't get me wrong. Don't try to develop some sort of convoluted backswing just so that you can emulate Jim Furyk or Matthew Wolff. They have a whole lot more athletic ability and hand-eye coordination than you do. They are talented enough to do weird things at the top and still be able to deliver the same consistent downswing. You are not. So, take the advice of the golf pro or the instructional book or the video analysis of your swing that shows you the optimal place for your golf club, hands, hips, feet etc. during your backswing. But don't get caught up in trying to make it perfect. Principle number one is to remember that we are simply trying to generate a swing that will consistently deliver the clubface to the back of the ball in a repeating fashion.

THE GRIP

Remember that part in the introduction where I told you that I wasn't going to spend time on general principles that are taught to you by the professional that are universally applicable and don't have anything to do with the special techniques you use to compensate for your lack of hand-eye coordination? Well, I lied. But just a little bit. It is necessary that we start out with a topic that is taught by every single pro. It's a technique that is universally applicable. In other words, it's one thing that you can do just as well as the pro. But it is important to stress it here, because it is such a fundamental factor of success. In other words, if you don't get this one right, none of the other techniques that I'm going to give you have any chance of success. I'm talking about the grip.

The emphasis of this book is on areas of the game where the abilities or lack thereof of a high-handicap golfer differ from the instructions given to a good professional or amateur golfer. The grip used in golf is one of the few areas where the techniques employed by the professionals and even the worst golfer are the same. However, no golf instructional book can be complete without an emphasis on using a proper grip.

However, many golf instructional books written by professionals can get overly technical and complicated. So, my goal in this book is to make the proper grip as easy to understand as possible.

Why is the golf grip so important? There are primarily two reasons. First, the grip is the only place where your body actually makes contact with the club. Therefore, it is the primary point at which you have the ability to control what the rest of the club is doing. Second, the grip is one of the few opportunities where, prior to swinging the club, you can influence what the club does. For example, by altering your grip between a weak grip, a neutral grip, and a strong grip, you can dramatically control how open or closed the clubface is when it makes contact with the ball.

The pressure of your grip also dramatically influences the type of shot that you hit. If your grip is too tight, especially if there is lots of tension in your arms, it can slow your clubhead speed. If you tighten up your grip in the backswing or downswing after you have already set the bottom edge of the clubface square with the ball, your grip pressure can cause the clubface to close, resulting in a shot to the left of the green (or to the right if you are a southpaw).

The main point about the grip is that it is one of the areas of the golf swing where you can be totally "locked and loaded" prior to beginning the swing. Most of your movements during the swing, such as the position of your lower body, where your elbows go during the shot, how far back you swing the club, etc. are determined in a split second. But with the grip, you have time during that moment of calm before beginning the swing to make sure that you get it right.

One of the best indicators of the importance of getting the grip right is the importance placed upon it by one of the greatest golf instructors of all time, Harvey Penick. If asked what golf professional won more total tournaments, most people would guess Tiger Woods, Sam Snead, Jack Nicklaus, or Ben Hogan. I'm afraid that you would just be showing your chauvinism. The winningest golf professional of all time was actually Kathy Whitworth with eighty-eight wins on the Ladies Professional Golf Association. When Kathy Whitworth first visited Harvey Penick, she said that he spent the entire first day on teaching her the golf grip. So, I guess that the greatest golf instructor of all time thought that the grip was pretty important.

First, as every golfer probably knows, there are three basic golf grips. The first is the overlapping grip. In this grip, the hand that is lower on the club (the right hand for a right-handed golfer) is snug up against the hand at the top of the grip.

The Overlapping Grip

The little finger of the lower hand actually lays between the index finger and the middle finger of the upper hand. This is the most preferred grip by professionals. It ensures that the two hands are working together without either hand overpowering the other.

The second grip is the interlocking grip. In this grip, the little finger of the lower hand actually goes underneath the index finger and out between the index finger and the middle finger of the upper hand. This grip is preferred by golfers with smaller hands. It tends to give more power to the hands, as they are more closely connected.

The Interlocking Grip

The third grip is the baseball or ten finger grip. The club is gripped, quite simply, the same way that you would grip a baseball bat. The upper and lower hands touch each other, but they are not connected. New golfers who are unfamiliar with the interlocking and overlapping grip tend to start out with a baseball grip, simply because they don't know the alternatives. The fact that virtually no one continues to use the baseball grip as they become better at the game should tell you something. So, if you are still using the baseball grip, you should experiment with either the overlapping grip or the interlocking grip.

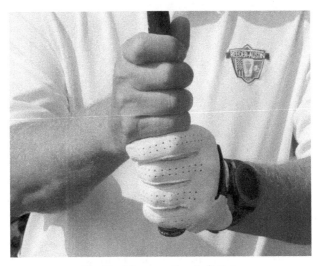

The Ten Finger or Baseball Grip

In taking your grip, begin by placing the upper hand (the left hand for a right-handed golfer) at the top of the club. But, in somewhat of an unnatural move, you do not want to grip the club in the palm of your hand. This is one of the main errors that beginning golfers and bad golfers make. That's the way you grip a baseball bat or a tennis racket. It just feels like a more natural way to hold the club. But instead, you want the club to fall in the fingers of the hand. As you look down at your upper hand, the club should fall in the fleshy part of the index finger between the first and second knuckles. It will fall more toward the palm of the hand in your middle, ring, and eventually, little finger.

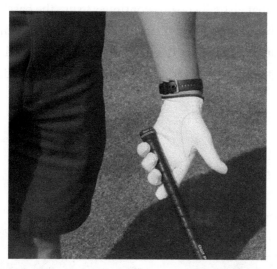

In the correct grip, notice how the club goes through fingers, not the palm of your hand. Once you have the club in your fingers, you can wrap the hand around the club and add the other hand.

Why do you want the club in the fingers, rather than in the palm of your hand? Well, as I pledged to you in the introduction, I don't want to get too technical. The purpose of this book is to keep golf instruction as simple as possible. But let me just illustrate with an analogy that you can relate to. If you want to pitch a baseball, where do you hold the ball? Do you throw the ball from the palm of your hand? No, in order to throw the most accurate and powerful pitch, you put the ball up into your index and middle fingers. The baseball is further stabilized by your ring and little fingers. Not only does this give the ball more stability and accuracy, but the lever effect that you get when your fingers snap forward gives more speed to your fastball. So, without a further technical explanation, you'll just have to take my word on this one. Starting your grip out with the club resting in your fingers will give you much more accuracy and power in your swing.

Next, add your lower hand to the club. Either interlock or place your little finger next to the index and middle fingers of your upper hand. Now we have to think about where the hands are on the club.

Basically, you have three different ways to grip the club. These are weak, neutral, or strong. Before we describe each of these, let's understand the basic reason that the position of the hands on the club is so important. Remember this. Your hands always return to a neutral position. What do we mean by that? What that means is that you can twist and turn your

The Weak Grip. Notice that the V's formed between the thumbs and the index fingers are pointing to the shoulder closest to the flag.

hands in whatever direction you want to. But when you swing the club down, your hands naturally gravitate toward a neutral position with both hands side by side in front of you. It's just a physiological fact. You can try to keep your grip strong or weak, but that just gives you one more thing to think about. Don't think about it. Just let this natural motion happen.

So, how does this affect the most important thing that the grip is determining, which is where the clubface is in relation to the ball when contact is made? Well, first, let's define the three types of grips. The first type of grip is a weak grip. A weak grip means that the hands are set with the grip twisted more around the club toward the target.

The second type of grip is the neutral grip. This means that the hands are neutral on the club with the front hand and the rear or lower hand facing each other on the club.

The Neutral Grip. The V's are pointed directly towards your head.

The third type of grip is the strong grip. In the strong grip, the hands are rotated around toward the back of the grip as you face the target.

The Strong Grip. The V's are pointed between your head and the trailing shoulder. Notice how you can now see two or three fingers in your forward hand.

The main way to determine what type of grip you have is by looking at the Vs formed by the thumb and the index fingers. Here is a quick tip to help determine where the Vs are pointed. Place two golf tees where the base of your thumb contacts the base of your index finger on both hands. After you take your grip, look at where those tees are pointing. First, if they are pointing in different directions, you've got a problem. Your hands are working at odds against each other. Ideally, you want the tees to both be pointing in the same direction.

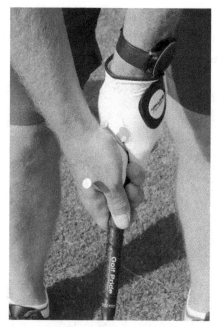

*Here is how to use the "tees in the V's" technique
to see what kind of grip you have.*

If you have a weak grip, your tees are going to be pointing somewhere between the side of your head and the front shoulder that is closest to the pin. If you have a neutral grip, the tees tend to be pointing at your head. If you have a strong grip, the tees will be pointing between the side of your head and your shoulder that is farther away from the pin (the right shoulder for a right-handed golfer).

There is a second way to determine what type of grip you have. That is to count the number of fingers you can see in your front (gloved) hand. In a strong grip, you should be able to see at least two or three fingers. With a neutral grip, you will probably see just your index finger. With a weak grip, odds are good that your front hand is twisted so far around the grip that you don't see any fingers at all.

What are the effects of the three types of grips? The effect of the grip on your shot was dramatically revealed to me in my very first golf lesson. Like the vast majority of first-time golfers and high-handicap golfers, I had a tendency to slice the ball. In my first golf lesson, the pro said, "I can fix that in a matter of minutes." I have to say, I was quite skeptical. After years of banana balls, I had concluded that there was no miracle cure.

While he made some other minor changes to my stance and swing plane, the main thing that he did was to move my hands around to a strong grip. My next shot screamed down the center of the fairway. How does this work? Well, remember my overriding comment about how the hands always return to a neutral position. Perhaps you would think that if you started with a neutral grip, and the hands always return to a neutral position, then your clubface should be in a neutral position when it contacts the ball. But that's where physics come into play. When the amateur golfer takes a backswing, the clubface tends to open up. You'll have to ask Isaac Newton why the natural centrifugal force opens up the clubface. But if you've been a lifelong slicer, you just know that it happens. And the problem is that the high-handicap golfer does not have the knowledge or the hand strength to be able to twist the club back so that it is neutral when it makes contact with the ball. Instead, the clubface remains open and ends up with the dreaded slice.

So, your body needs a little bit of help. If you set up with the clubface in a neutral position directly behind the ball, but then rotate the hands back into a strong grip, when you swing down with your downswing, the hands will twist back to a neutral position. This has the effect of closing the clubface. You do not realize it, but the hands which were turned to the right (for a right-handed golfer) now rotate back into a neutral position (where the Vs of the grip would now point more toward your head), closing the clubface which had opened during the backswing.

If a strong grip is needed by the average golfer to return the clubface to a neutral position and avoid the slice, why would you ever have to consider a weak grip? It's because there are some gorillas out there. There are golfers out there whose natural hand strength tends to twist the club around so that the clubface is closed or turned in when it makes contact with the ball. This results in those duck hooks down the left side (for a right-handed golfer). They need to compensate in the opposite direction. By taking a weak grip with the tees pointing to the forward shoulder, when that strong golfer twists their hands back to a neutral position, it offsets the tendency to close the clubface, resulting in a nice neutral position of the clubface when it contacts the ball.

You will generally find that your strong grip is needed for the driver and maybe the fairway metals, but not so much for your iron shots. Frankly, it has to do with the size of the club head. The driver, with its larger head, is simply harder for the average golfer to close during their downswing. The irons are easier to rotate during the downswing. So, a neutral grip, or even a weak grip for the gorillas among us, is more common for the grip of your irons.

STANCE

Maybe I lied a little more than I thought, because there is a second fundamental element of golf that is universally applicable, but needs to be emphasized in this book. That is having a proper stance. I'm not going to spend too much time on this topic, as it is thoroughly covered in golf instructional books and videos and by the golf instructor. But, like the grip, a good stance is absolutely essential to a good golf shot. If you don't get the stance right, you can take all of the compensatory, mechanical steps to ensure that you make solid contact with the ball, but your results are going to be poor. So, let's talk about the stance.

The stance is another area where we can replicate the pro. The instructional books and videos generally tell us to take an athletic stance. You'll usually find a photo of a shortstop. But not all shortstops are created equally. Pros argue over the level of knee bend. I actually read two articles in the same issue of a golf magazine. One said to bend your knees quite a bit, like a shortstop. The other article said that that was old school advice. In the modern golf game, it was better to stay upright with not too much knee bend. If you look at a pro like

Will Zalatoris, his legs are almost ramrod straight. And even though he doesn't have much meat on his bones, he's one of the longest drivers on the pro tour. So, the magazine reader is reading two conflicting pieces of advice in the same issue. No wonder we are all confused!

So, my advice is to forget all that. Head out to the driving range. Start with a slight knee bend. Your main thought is to keep the backbone straight. Don't hunch over. Feel like your butt is sticking out. Your head should be erect and not slumped over at the neck. Start out with an old school, short-stop-oriented knee bend. See how you hit the ball. Then try straightening your legs. Does it make you better or worse? At the end of the day, stick with what works best for you.

But let me share a little secret with you. At the end of the day, your level of knee flex probably has very little to do with how you play golf. It's probably very important to someone who plays at the level of a professional. But for you, the most important thing is to make solid contact with the ball. How much or little you flex your knees probably doesn't have a whole lot to do with that. Sure, if you are standing ramrod straight, and it is creating tension in your body, this will negatively impact your ability to make solid contact with the ball. But, as long as you remain loose and relaxed and confident, knee flex is probably not that critical. Simply find a position in which you are comfortable in making that all-important repeating swing.

On the other hand, the upper body portion of your stance is a bit more critical. What you do with your upper body does significantly affect your ability to make that elusive solid contact with the ball. In order for you to envision the position in which your upper body should be, a visual symbol is important. When you think about your spine and its relationship to the ball, think of the hinging of a door. The purpose of the hinge is to swing open and then swing shut. And that's exactly what you want your upper body to do. But have you ever seen a hinge that was bent over? If you did, it must've been an unhinged hinge. No, hinges are ramrod straight. And that's what you need your spine to be. If your spine is crooked or curved, it makes it very difficult for this opening of the hinge and closing of the hinge to take place.

So how do we create this effect of a straight spine? Well, let's start with your butt. People tend to have the tendency to allow their spines to curve forward just above the hips. But the hips are a critical part of the base of our hinged effect. What's the best way to ensure that our lower body at the base of our hinge is straight? The best advice is the old advice. When you set up, stick your butt out a bit. It may not be the position you want to be in for your prom picture, but it's the best way to ensure that your spine starts at the bottom nice and straight.

Keeping the spine straight through the gut area, the lungs, and the heart is pretty easy. Almost all of us can get that right. But the next problem child is the neck. If you served in the Marine Corps, you probably have ramrod straight posture. For the rest of us, we have a tendency to lean forward at the neck. This next piece of advice is very, very important. Don't get too wrapped up in trying to have your neck and head ramrod straight. If you do, you're probably going to be thinking about that during the shot. You're probably going to get tense in the shoulders and neck. Both of these things are not good for having a smooth repeating shot with solid contact. So, as one of the final things you do before you pull the trigger, feel that your butt is out and your spine is straight, and then totally forget about it.

It might look a little funny, but stick your rear end out and try to create a straight line in your spine from your butt through the top of your head. That's how the hinge technique works best.

As far as other advice on the stance, I'm going to stop right here. There are many other valuable tips that your pro or instructional book and video can offer, things such as letting your arms hang down straight versus being slightly extended. Or where to place your weight on certain shots. For chips and sand shots, you are commonly advised to place your weight on your front foot. But for your drive, a common technique to eke out a few more yards is having a K-shaped stance and leaning slightly on your back foot. Placing your weight on your front or back foot and where to place your arms are more of those universally applicable techniques where you want to follow what your pro advises. A good instructional book will give you all of the information you need on the other tips to improve your stance.

I'm also not going to get into where you place the ball in your stance. Again, these are universally applicable techniques. Placing your ball forward in your stance for your drive, a little bit farther back for your fairway metals, and in the middle of your stance for your irons is something that is the same for you and the pro. Our focus is on the things that you need to do that are different from what the pros do and teach.

For now, just focus on having a nice, relaxed stance, with a straight backbone that enables you to open the hinge and then close the hinge. Once you master those basics, you are ready to move on to the final step before initiating the shot itself.

THE PRE-SHOT
ROUTINE

Any golf instructional book or video or any lesson from a pro is going to stress the importance of the pre-shot routine. So, I'm not going to dwell too much on the routine or its need. Rather, I will simply relay to you some of the most effective techniques as they relate to the golfer with less than ideal hand-eye coordination.

Just in case you have been living under a rock, let me remind you what the pre-shot routine is. Obviously, pre-shot would refer to any mechanical steps that you take prior to hitting the ball. But the word routine implies that it is a similar action each time. And that's exactly what it is. Prior to hitting the ball, you want to go through the same sequence of events each time that you hit the ball. This is important from both a mental and physical perspective.

It's well established for all golfers, and especially for golfers lacking confidence in their swing, that the mental aspect of golf is very important to success. You may have heard the old saying that golf is a game of inches. Primarily, the six inches between your ears. Golf psychologists, like Bob Rotella, point out that even the worst golfers have the technical ability to swing the club back and through. They may not be able to hit a drive three hundred yards, but unless they have a severe physical limitation, virtually everyone is capable of advancing the golf ball down the middle of the fairway. So, if the physical barriers are not causing us to hit the ball in a huge banana, a screaming duck hook, popped up into the air, or dribbling down the fairway, then what is our barrier to a good golf game? The answer is our mental approach to the game.

Let's start with the mental benefits of a good pre-shot routine. When we say that the mental aspect of the game causes us to make a poor shot, we're not talking about mental aspect as related to intelligence, or the ability to intellectually understand the dynamics of a successful golf swing. Even people of very low intelligence can swing a long device back and through. It doesn't take a rocket scientist to figure out how to swing the golf club. No, the mental aspect is really more of a negative function than a positive function.

The negative mental aspect of the game is allowing so many doubts and thoughts to enter your brain that you are not able to focus on making solid contact with the ball. Remember, as a golfer who is not blessed with the greatest in hand-eye coordination, there are physical factors that are affecting your ability to catch the ball on the sweet spot. Professional golfers and good amateur golfers have the physical talent to be able to swing the club back and swing it through, catching the ball exactly where they want to on the face of the club. If you're reading this book, you probably don't have that same inherent talent.

Does that mean that this physical limitation prevents you from making a solid contact with the ball? No. You just have to work a bit harder at it. You are not able to do what the "feel-oriented" pros recommend, which is to swing the club through the downswing while simply letting the ball get in the way of the clubface. If you tried to do that, it would be a disaster. You would hit the ball on the toe of the clubface, on the hosel, on the bottom edge of the club and somewhere on the face of the club after it plowed through two inches of terra firma.

In order for you to make solid contact on the sweet spot of the club, you have to focus your total attention on the back of the ball. First, you can't do this if you lack the confidence that you are going to be able to pull it off. Second, you can't concentrate and totally focus on making solid contact with the ball if your mind is cluttered with all types of extraneous swing thoughts.

So, the first benefit of a good pre-shot routine is that it enhances your ability to focus on the task at hand. You have most likely met people who we graciously refer to as "creatures of habit." These are people who tend to do things the same way every time. It can get out of hand, such as people with obsessive-compulsive behavior. These are people who get very upset if items on the mantelpiece are not turned in exactly the right direction. No, I am simply referring to the inherent ability to focus when we are performing a task that we have performed many, many times.

Let's say that you are fixing your cup of morning coffee. It's something that you have done thousands of times over the years. There's not a whole lot of suspense about what you do. You go through basically the same steps every morning. But let's say that one morning, you decided to deviate from your normal habit. You decided that maybe you should brew the coffee for a little bit longer or a little bit shorter than normal. Now you find yourself asking questions such as, "How long should I brew the coffee?" "Should I add more or less water than I normally do?" What is your brain now doing? It is bringing in the element of indecision. That's exactly what you don't want to have happen as you're standing over the ball.

Through repetitive practice, you want to ingrain in your brain exactly the technique that you want to use in hitting the ball. If this is properly done, then when you stand over the ball, you will be totally focused on the technique that you have now used hundreds or thousands of times. You won't be asking yourself questions about various alternatives to your standard methodology. And that technique begins with a tried-and-true series of events. Those series of events are your pre-shot routine.

The second mental benefit of the pre-shot routine is that it gives you confidence in the shot. This confidence is generally built on the driving range. When you go to the driving range, do you simply stand over a bucket of balls and hit shot after shot with no focus on target, direction, or any factors you will encounter on the course? If so, you're making one of the worst confidence building mistakes that you can make.

Instead, you should go through your entire pre-shot routine before every shot on the range. Why? Well, if you perform the same physical function over and over again, you're probably going to perform better than under normal circumstances. If you hit one good shot with your seven iron, roll up another ball, and hit the seven iron again, you are most likely to repeat that good shot. Our muscles are ingrained from the previous successful shot. Our confidence is high that were going to hit the shot well. But that's not the way it works on the course.

You don't move immediately from one seven iron shot to another. So, you are giving your mind and body a false benefit that you will find difficult to replicate out on the course.

Instead, what you want to do is approach each shot as a separate shot, just like you do on the actual golf course. Start out behind the ball with your pre-shot routine, work your way up to the ball, and hit a great shot. When you do this, you are developing the confidence that you can initiate a shot in isolation, and not simply through rote activity. Therefore, you can see once you hit the course that if you execute your pre-shot routine and step up to the ball and are able to hit it consistently on the range, then this same confidence in your shot will carry itself through to the actual game.

I mentioned that the benefits of the pre-shot routine are both mental and physical. What is the physical benefit of a good pre-shot routine? It comes down to the concept of muscle memory. You'll hear that term a lot. I hate to burst any bubbles, but your muscles actually don't really have memories. Memory is a function of the brain. Muscles don't have a brain. Therefore, your muscle doesn't have the ability to remember something that it learned an hour ago.

But it's the darndest thing. Even though muscles don't have a brain, and therefore do not have the ability to remember something, muscles can be trained to do repetitive activities. Sometimes this can get a little creepy. I recall as a young child watching my grandmother as she slept. Her hands were moving while she slept! I asked my mother about it. She said that my grandmother was "knitting in her sleep." My grandmother had knitted so much in her life that the muscles in her hands were subconsciously moving in the manner in which they had been trained.

We probably won't have you physically playing golf in your sleep. However, I must confess that I am guilty of taking an imaginary golf swing in public. I remember practicing my golf swing while standing and waiting to retrieve my luggage from an airline flight. I vividly remember the expression on people's faces when I looked up from my practice reverie. I suppose I did look a little strange. But be honest. You have probably taken a few practice golf swings of your own in public. That's not a bad thing. That's a function of training your muscles to perform the physical requirements of a good golf swing, just like a concert pianist trains their fingers to tickle the ivories.

But there's another aspect of muscle memory. While the scientists struggle to understand why this happens, it's a proven fact that muscles tend to repeat a physical function more effectively for a few seconds after that physical function has been performed. You have most likely witnessed this yourself. If you step up to any virtually complex physical function ice cold, your chances of doing it effectively are reduced. However, if you practice that physical motion several times, and then immediately perform it, your ability to execute it effectively is enhanced. Therefore, the practice swing is a fundamental part of the pre-shot routine. Or at least it should be for you.

There are many pre-shot routines that you can utilize. But allow me to suggest a specific routine that will benefit you as a "mechanical" golfer. First, start out behind the ball. Obviously, you will need to make your pre-shot club selection prior to beginning your pre-shot routine. Find out the yardage to the hole. Look for extraneous circumstances, such as is the green elevated or lowered. Throw the little tufts of grass into the air (trying to look as much as possible like a golf professional). Gauge how hard the wind is blowing and in which direction it is blowing. Determine whether or not the weather will affect your distance. Cold thick air will cause your balls to not go as far. Balls go farther in hot dry air. Factor in your elevation. Golfers playing in the Rocky Mountains soon learn that their ball goes a lot farther in thin air. Determine what kind of roll you're going to get. Is the ground wet and saturated? Or is it hot and dry?

Once you have analyzed all of these factors from behind the ball, and not while standing over the ball, make your club selection. This is very important. Once you've made your club selection, tell your brain that it is the perfect club selection. There is no possible scenario under which a different club would produce a better result. You are totally committed to the effectiveness of the club that you have selected.

Now you are ready to begin your routine. Standing behind the ball, select your target. As you know, this may not always be as simple as hitting the ball to the middle of the green. For most of your shots, that's going to be the ideal target. Don't try to be a hero. Jack Nicklaus can go for the pin that is placed six paces in from the right side of the green. But you're not Jack Nicklaus. Aim for the center of the green. If you pull the ball or push the ball, you've still got a good chance of getting on the green and being able to putt for par.

But are you always hitting to the center of the green? Not necessarily. What if, despite your best efforts, you have the tendency to fade or draw your approach shots. I play with a golfer who has always drawn his approach shots dramatically. His ball will easily move thirty feet from right to left. But he factors this into his setup. Golfers who play with him for the first time think he's going to hit the ball way off to the right of the green. Instead, his iron shots take off to the right, turn, and land like a butterfly right in the middle of the green. So, if constant practice has shown you that you have one of these idiosyncrasies, then factor that into your choice of target.

Once you have determined your target, use the age-old technique of finding something on the ground six to twelve inches in front of your ball. It may be a leaf. It may be an imperfection in the grass. It doesn't really matter. What if the imperfection isn't right online toward your target? Not a problem. Just say to yourself, "I want to line up my shot two inches to the right of that tuft of grass." Lining up your ball is critically important. First, it aids you in hitting the ball in the direction that you want it to go. However, the second benefit may be even more important. It enables you to convince your brain that your ball is going to go where you want it to go. That's all about having confidence in the golf shot.

So far, I probably haven't told you anything that you are not already doing. You most likely analyze the factors affecting your shot and make your club selection. You most likely know to line up your shot toward the target. But this next suggestion may be new to you.

Take your grip while standing behind the ball. Why? If you watch most amateur golfers, you will see that they don't take their grip until they are standing over the ball. Why is this a mistake? First, let's go back to that matter of confidence. If you take your grip while still standing behind the ball, that is one more check mark that you can use to convince your brain that you are about to hit one of the best shots you've ever hit. Again, it's all about confidence and focus. You want to have the confidence and you want to be able to have the focus on the ball that will lead to an effective golf shot. You don't want to be thinking about whether or not you have your grip correct.

The next benefit of taking your grip behind the ball is more utilitarian. Have you ever established your aiming spot in front of the ball, gotten over the ball and started fiddling with your grip, only to forget which spot is the one that you are aiming for? Come on. Admit it. You've done it before. If you watch a pro, if they lose their spot, what do they do? They step back behind the ball and start their pre-shot routine all over. But they are playing for millions of dollars!

Why don't you do that? Because you are sensitive to the fact that you are not the greatest golfer in the world. So, your thought process is, "Well, I may not be the best golfer in the world, but I'm at least not going to be the slowest golfer." You simply don't want to hold up everyone by taking the time to step back and start your routine all over again. So, what do you do? You simply decide to go ahead and take your swing even though you're not sure of the direction in which it will go. What's that going to do to you? Create an off-line shot, but more importantly, force you into making a shot that you are not confident that you will hit effectively. Therefore, go ahead and lock in on your grip while still standing behind the ball.

Next, you want to take your practice swing before you get up beside the ball. Watch the pros. Where did they take their practice swing? Almost always behind the ball. Why is that? Believe it or not, there's a certain element of ego involved. I once listened to a very famous pro talking about the first time that he played with an equally famous, but older pro. After the round, he said that the older pro came up to him and congratulated him on the quality of his play. But his departing words were, "But lose the practice swing."

I don't know if it's the feeling that taking one or more practice swings prior to hitting the ball is making you that slow golfer that I discussed earlier. Maybe it's the fear that you might accidentally hit your ball with your practice swing. Come on. Admit it. You've probably done that too. You might remember when Davis Love III accidentally hit his ball on the green while practicing his putt. It sent thousands of golfers to the rulebook to determine whether or not he replaced the ball where it originally had been, hit it from its new location, or took a penalty. So, it can happen to the best of golfers. This leads many golfers to decide not to take the chance and to avoid the practice swing after they step up to the ball.

There's one more good reason to take the practice swing behind the ball. Maybe it's psychological, but I think that the amateur golfer can approach the swing with more confidence after taking their practice swing as part of their pre-shot routine. Watch the golf professionals when they take their practice swing. Whether they make one practice swing or multiple swings, after they take that swing, they lurch forward to immediately take their stance over the ball. You can see the confidence in their eyes. It's almost as if that practice swing was the signal that they were ready to make the best swing of their life. Again, it's all about confidence.

Now watch the poor amateur prior to hitting the ball. Standing beside the ball, they take one or more practice swings. You can almost read it in their eyes. They're wondering if this swing is even going to work. They are thinking about dozens of other things, such as are their feet wide enough apart, is their elbow close enough to their body, or are they taking the club back too far or too short. After their final practice swing, as they step six inches closer to the ball, you can see that their confidence level is about as low as it can be.

So, which situation would you rather be in? The confident pro who takes a few swings behind the ball just to ingrain that muscle memory and then steps over the ball with total confidence in their swing? Or the amateur who takes a couple of wishy-washy practice swings and steps over the ball looking like hitting the ball is the last thing on earth that they want to do? Maybe it's psychological. But isn't that what the whole mental aspect of golf is all about? For me, it comes down to the fact that the people who are swinging a golf club for a living and the potential to make millions of dollars almost all take their practice swings behind the ball.

But regardless of where you choose to take your practice swing, your next step is to take your stance over the ball.

Begin the pre-shot routine from behind the ball. Note that I have already taken my grip. While taking your full practice swing, locate an aiming spot just in front of your ball. Finally, visualize the shot. Now you are ready to step up to the ball.

Now, we get to the next most essential element of the pre-shot routine. That's the waggle. If you saw the movie *Tin Cup*, you remember that having a waggle was a critical part of Kevin Costner's instruction for René Russo. Granted, he had a little bit more extracurricular activity in mind than simply preparing her to hit the best shot. But it doesn't diminish the fact that virtually every golf instructor is going to stress the importance of a good waggle.

The waggle may be simply bringing the golf club away from the ball and back up behind the ball. It might be a series of small movements to relax the wrists. You might remember that Sergio Garcia went through a phase where he would make about twenty of these small movements. He got a lot of abuse for that. So, I don't recommend making your waggle into a major production.

The waggle might be pulling the golf club back into sort of a half swing as you focus on bringing the golf club back on plane and with the right tempo. Or you will see good golfers bring the clubface all the way back into a full backswing. Clearly, they are integrating the muscle memory into their arms and hips to remember things like not taking the club past parallel or keeping the trail arm elbow close into their midsection. Regardless of what sort of waggle you have as part of your pre-shot routine, you want to have a waggle and you want to do the same waggle with every shot.

The benefit of the waggle is, of course, to relieve tension in your forearms and hands. The longer you stand over a shot, the more tense you tend to get. As we all know, tension is the enemy of a good golf shot. So, use the waggle to loosen up the muscles and relieve the tension in the arms.

Can your waggle vary from shot to shot? Yes. Earlier, I said that you should have the same waggle with every shot. What I mean is that you should have the same waggle for every drive every time you hit a seven iron and every time you hit a pitch shot. Does that mean that you have to have the same waggle technique with your driver as you do with your wedge? Of course not. When driving the ball, the pros tend to do a little waggle or practice bringing the clubhead back on plane and with good tempo. They don't do multiple waggles.

But watch a professional prior to hitting a chip shot. They may take a half dozen practice swings. Part of that is gauging the conditions. The thickness of the grass is the primary consideration. But also, because the wedge shot is one of the most technique-oriented shots that we will hit, they want to ingrain some serious muscle memory into their body so that they can immediately replicate the shot that they have designed to achieve the best result. So, feel free to have a different waggle, depending on the circumstances of the shot, but as a confidence builder, try to take the same waggle with each shot of the same club.

At long last, you are ready to hit the ball. But you are now hitting the ball with the greatest degree of confidence and focus. First, you have completely analyzed the situation to determine the best club selection, shot shape, etc. Secondly, you have found a visual cue to line up your shot so that you have the greatest chances of hitting it in the direction in which you want it to go. Third, you've taken a practice swing to ingrain muscle memory for the next few seconds to convince your brain that your practice swing is as perfect as possible and that your odds of replicating that with the ball in the way are as high as possible. Fourth, you have stepped up to the ball with a sense of confidence and mission. Fifth, you have taken a waggle to lessen the tension in your arms and hands and to achieve that final degree of muscle memory. If you follow this recommended pre-shot routine, you will be well on your way to hitting the best shot possible.

THE SWING
IN GENERAL

In discussing techniques related to the different types of clubs, there are many elements of the swing that are similar. But then there are elements that are unique to that type of club or shot. We've already discussed several of the techniques of a good swing. For example, we discussed that the overall objective of your swing is to consistently swing the club the same way every time. Regardless of what you do with the club and the clubface during your backswing and downswing, if you are able to consistently deliver a neutral clubface to the back of the ball with every swing, your game is going to improve dramatically.

Secondly, we've discussed the importance of the hinge principle. Your swing doesn't have to have a whole lot of moving parts. If your body simply swings back like a hinge that is opening and then swings back through like a hinge that is closing, it will significantly increase your odds of making solid contact with the ball.

Now let's discuss a few other simple principles of a solid contact, repeating swing. First, we are going to talk about the importance of keeping your arms close to your body. If you go to a pro, they are going to emphasize the importance of keeping your arms close to your body. But the importance in doing so is magnified for a high-handicap golfer. One of the most popular drills taught by the pros involves placing a golf glove, towel, or similar object under one or both armpits. If the golfer allows the arms, especially the back arm, to sway away from the body, the towel or glove falls to the ground. The golf pro uses this drill as a very effective way to show you that your arms have disconnected from your body. If you want to know why keeping your arms close to the body makes for a better golf shot, you can read it in any golf instructional book, or your golf pro can explain the physics of the situation.

At minimum, place a towel or golf glove under the armpit of your trailing arm. If you have a long enough towel or more than one glove, place them under both armpits.

*Then take your practice swing. If you are keeping your arms
properly connected to your body, the towel or gloves will
remain tucked under your armpits.*

But for establishing a solid contact golf shot for the hand-eye coordination challenged golfer, this simple technique becomes much more important. Because you struggle with returning the clubface directly behind the ball, you tend to thud the clubface into the ground behind the ball. As you know, that's called hitting the ball fat. Or the leading edge of the club hits the ball somewhere around the equator of the ball. That's called hitting the ball thin. Or you may contact the ball on the tip of the clubface. That causes that weak little shot that goes off to the side about halfway to the hole. Or you might hit the ball off the hosel of the club. We are not even going to mention what that's called. The bottom line is that you struggle to return the clubface back to where it collides with the ball in the center of the clubface.

So, you need to utilize physics in order to consistently strike the back of the ball. That's where the pendulum effect comes in. I'm sure that you've seen a pendulum before. Any object that has a weight on the end of a string or chain exhibits the pendulum effect. But here's the neat thing about a pendulum. As long as that string or chain is anchored to a constant location, the ball or other object at the other end of the string or the chain is always the same distance from the anchor. It can't get farther or closer from where the string or chain is anchored.

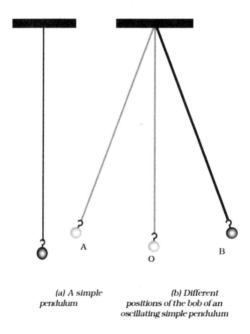

(a) A simple pendulum

(b) Different positions of the bob of an oscillating simple pendulum

The pendulum effect is critical to a successful golf shot. Keep your anchor point constant and the club always comes back to where it started.

You want to create the same effect in your golf swing. So, what you have to do is to anchor your arm just like a pendulum. You're going to do that in two ways. For a short shot using your short irons, where power is less important than accuracy, you are going to use your elbow as the anchor. For longer shots where you don't have the luxury of anchoring your elbow to your body throughout the entire shot, such as long irons, fairway metals, or the driver, you're going to use your shoulder as the anchor point.

These are the basic principles of the golf swing. We will look at the tips that are unique to each of the types of clubs as we go through each type of club individually.

TEMPO AND RHYTHM

Two of the most important factors in the quality of your golf swing are tempo and rhythm. Most golfers have a vague idea of what they refer to but are not really sure what the difference is between the two. So, first, let us define the terms. The difference is subtle, but there is a difference.

Tempo refers to the overall speed with which you swing the club. Some golfers, such as Nick Price and Bryson DeChambeau, are known for swinging very quickly. If you blink while Bryson DeChambeau is swinging, you'll probably miss it. On the other hand, other golfers, such as Fred Couples and Ernie Els, are known for their slower swing motion.

Rhythm, on the other hand, refers to the sequence of movement within the golf swing. There are a lot of moving parts in the golf swing. Some movements are linear. For example, the clubhead has to go back before it can go forward. However, there are many movements that are taking place simultaneously. For example, slow-motion footage of some of the best golfers shows that their hips begin to fire forward while they are still completing their backswing.

We may assume that if two golfers have a different tempo, then they have a different rhythm. But slow-motion video shows just the opposite. A golfer like Rickie Fowler might have a very fast tempo, while a golfer like Ernie Els might have a slower tempo. However, slow-motion video reveals that they both have a very similar rhythm. In other words, regardless of the speed with which one completes their backswing and downswing, the order in which their various movements occur can be very similar.

A lot of high-handicap golfers assume that you have to have a very quick tempo to your golf swing in order to hit the ball far. But have you ever noticed that Ernie Els and Fred Couples hit the ball a long way? Another erroneous assumption that high-handicap golfers make is that the backswing and the downswing have to be at the same tempo. If this were true, golfers such as Ernie Els, who swings back with a slow, easy tempo would not hit the ball very far because their downswing would replicate this slow tempo. In other words, their swing would be so slow that it does not generate the clubhead speed typical of a golfer like Ernie Els or Fred Couples.

What can we learn from the tempo and rhythm of these great golfers? The first thing to know is that you are not Nick Price, Bryson DeChambeau, or Rickie Fowler. These golfers can swing the club extremely rapidly and still make solid contact with the ball. Why? Because they have the incredible hand-eye coordination that you don't have. So, our first lesson learned is don't assume that you need to swing very rapidly in order to hit the ball a long way.

In order to grasp our next bit of learning, it is important to understand where the swing speed comes from. Ernie Els has a long easy backswing. So, where is he generating his clubhead speed? It's quite simple. He generates his speed from his downswing. In other words, just because a golfer takes a slow route to the top of their backswing doesn't mean that their downswing has to be slow. In fact, it's just the opposite. These golfers with a slower tempo use a more deliberate backswing, but generate incredible power as they swing through the ball.

So, your next tip is to emulate their swing tempo rather than the tempo of the fast golfers. Let me illustrate. This is a really dumb scenario which I am sure you will never face. But it really illustrates my point. Let's assume that someone told you that you had to stand with your hands on your hips. They are going to stand three feet in front of you holding a target. If you swing either one of your arms out and hit the target in exactly the middle of the bullseye, you will receive one million dollars. But if you miss the bullseye by the slightest amount, you will receive nothing. You can swing your arm at any speed you like. Would you swing your arm as rapidly as possible toward the target? Of course not. Your odds of making contact in the middle of the bullseye are rapidly diminished with the faster speed with which you swing your arm. You would most likely swing your arm slowly and deliberately toward the bullseye.

The same is true for the golf swing. The biggest problem with golfers assuming that they have to swing rapidly is that their lack of hand-eye coordination dramatically reduces their chances of catching the ball on the sweet spot when they swing the club rapidly. But you can only carry that so far. Obviously, you have to generate a decent level of clubhead speed in order to progress the ball down the fairway.

So, what's the compromise? In order to have the maximum opportunity to make solid contact with the ball, what you want to do is have a slow and deliberate backswing that gives you the greatest odds of positioning the club in the optimal position at the top of your backswing. Once this position is achieved, then you want to fire your hips and generate as much speed as you can in your arms in the downswing of your driver and longer clubs. On your clubs where accuracy is more important than power and distance, such as your wedges and short irons, you're going to generate your downswing through your arms rather than your legs. But the same principle is still true. The best technique is a slower, more deliberate backswing to establish your short iron at the top of your backswing and then generate power as you swing through the ball.

As you know, the purpose of this book is to emphasize the techniques that high-handicap golfers need to utilize to compensate for their lack of hand-eye coordination and not to regurgitate universal precepts of good golf techniques that can be used by good and bad golfers alike. However, there is one universal training tip that I want to remind you of because it is so important to the concept that we are discussing. This tip is to take your golf club and hold it by the opposite end. Then take your swing.

For some odd reason, which I can't explain, the sound of the speed of your golf swing is more intense when the handle of the golf club is swinging through where the ball would be. This drill offers immediate feedback where, based on the sound that the club makes, you can tell when the clubhead is swinging faster or slower. There are lots of other golf swing aids that can do the same thing. You've seen the devices that actually measure the speed of your clubhead. There are swing trainers that can help you gauge the speed of your club. Regardless of which technique you use, your objective is to realize that the downswing and the backswing can be done at two different tempos. Your goal, through practice, is to get to the point where you use a slow and deliberate backswing to get into the optimal position at the top, and then to initiate as much speed on the downswing as you can generate and still make solid contact with the ball.

For some funny reason, you can "hear" the speed of your swing better if you grip the club by the clubhead and swing the club with the handle going through the air.

As for rhythm, your objective is to develop a rhythm in your swing that is consistent from shot to shot. One of the best techniques for this is the good old-fashioned wall mirror. Stand in front of the mirror and execute your golf swing in slow motion. Break down what is happening with each of your body parts. Where are your elbows during certain parts of the swing? Where is your club at the top? Is it at parallel, short of parallel, or past parallel? What are you doing with your hips once you are ready to generate the downswing?

Once you've looked at all of the different elements of the swing in super slow motion, begin to speed up a bit, putting all of the movements together. Focus on moving from one motion to the next in a smooth rhythmical fashion.

Most amateur golfers don't suffer from the problem of swinging too slowly. Their problem is that they tend to swing too quickly. In addition to swinging too quickly, they also have a tendency to jerk from one motion to the next. So, the first solution is quite easy. SLOW DOWN. Granted, if you slow down your swing, you probably won't hit any three hundred-yard drives. But I'm guessing that if you're reading this book, that's not your objective. If you have a handicap of fifteen or more, a more worthy objective is to get to the point where you're hitting drives two hundred to two hundred and fifty yards down the middle of the fairway. The way to do that is to slow down your backswing, generate your clubhead speed during your downswing, and allow your elements of your swing to progress in a coordinated, rhythmical fashion.

Here's one final tip on rhythm. I like to volunteer at various professional golf tournaments. I generally work as a walking scorer. This gives me the opportunity to get "inside the ropes" and watch how the good guys do it. One of the things that amazes me, which you don't always see on television, is how much the best golfers in the world practice their swing in between shots. While they are waiting to hit, they fold their arms across their chest like a mummy and slowly and deliberately take a simulated backswing and downswing.

Then, they address an imaginary ball with an imaginary club. Slowly and deliberately, they swing the club to the top and then down through the ball. The key word here is slowly. Even though these professional golfers have hit the ball thousands, if not millions of times, they still take frequent opportunities to slowly progress through the sequences of the swing. Are they working on their tempo? Obviously not. They are swinging at a much slower tempo than they normally would. What they are working on is their rhythm. They're working on continually training their body to swing in a rhythmical fashion. You should do the same.

With these universally applicable technique reminders out of the way, let's now get to the reason you bought this book. We're going to go club by club and shot by shot, learning the techniques that you can use to make solid contact with the ball.

THE WEDGE SHOT

If you ask golfers what is the most difficult shot to pull off, you'll get a variety of answers. Interestingly enough, you'll get completely different answers from pros and good amateur players and high-handicap players. From high-handicap golfers, you will get a lot of answers related to the long irons. Whereas a high-handicap golfer begins sweating just looking at a three iron, pros hit them with the greatest of ease. For pros, shots that require technique are not as imposing. That's because they spend hours every day working on their technique. Their answer to the question generally focuses on shots that require more mental technique.

For amateurs, physical technique tends to be more of a problem. For example, one of the primary answers for high-handicap golfers is the sand shot. Listen to a high-handicap golfer who just hit the ball into the sand. You would think that they just lost their long-lost love. But pros and good amateurs don't tend to fear the sand shots. In fact, you've probably heard pros say that they would rather be in the greenside bunker than in the grass on the fringe. That's especially true if the grass is tall or thick. Why? Because pros and good amateurs have mastered the technique of getting out of the bunker.

But perhaps the most universal answer among all golfers is the wedge shot. Whether the wedge is being used for a lob shot or a chip, the wedge is generally considered the hardest shot in golf. I believe that the reason for this is that technique can only take you so far. How many times have you read an article in one of the golf magazines in which they provided you the perfect technique for hitting a thirty-yard lob shot, only to go out and totally butcher the shot?

While the mental game is important for every shot, the difference between the mental aspect of hitting a drive is completely different from the mental aspect of hitting a chip. It all comes down to margin of error. With your drive, I'm sure you go through all the mental duress. If you didn't, you wouldn't be reading this book! But the mental exercise on the tee is related more to panic about where the shot is going. Will the old banana slice come out? Will I duck hook the drive? Although we are all capable of topping the ball off the tee, I don't find that's generally high on the list of the high-handicapper's fears. If the golfer is topping the ball, the techniques in the golf magazines generally can address them.

So, what separates the mental aspect of hitting a wedge shot from hitting a drive off the tee or a shot from the fairway? Margin of error. With a large driver, especially the outrageously large driver heads we have today, there is much more margin of error. Due to the gear effect, even if you don't catch the ball squarely in the sweet spot, it's still possible to hit a decent drive. With an iron shot, especially using the technique of coming down sharply on the back of the ball that we cover in the section on irons, you have a much wider margin of error. If you hit the ball fat, and take a nice divot, you will still advance the ball down the fairway. It may not go as far as you wanted it to, but, unless you catch a fairway bunker, greenside bunker, or some other hazard, you still have a shot from which you can recover. If you hit the ball thin, it's the opposite effect. Strangely enough, thin shots can actually end up going about the same distance as the shot you intended to hit. They may do it a little differently, killing many gophers along the way, but I've seen many a golfer hit a seven iron 140 yards with the ball never clearing the height of their head.

But then we get to the wedges. When hitting a lob shot with a wedge, you might be using a technique similar to the rest of your irons. If you're trying to hit a pitching wedge ninety to one hundred yards, you would use a technique very similar to hitting your seven iron. Therefore, what we're referring to would be shots from fifty yards and in. With those shots, you generally don't attempt to hit a very descending shot with a large divot. Some of us do it, mostly by accident. Instead, the technique tends to be a shot where the clubface slides neatly under the ball. That's where the margin of error difference comes in. That's because the width between the top of the grass and the bottom of the ball is very small. If you're playing on a really nice golf course with lush green grass, your margin of error could be as much as having the ball teed up. But if you're playing on your local muni during the winter or early spring, you might as well be hitting off your driveway. Your margin of error is reduced to a quarter of an inch or less.

Now we get to the double whammy of why the wedge shot is so hard to hit. First, it's just darned hard to hit! If you don't return the club back to that quarter to half an inch sliver, you either hit the ball fat or thin. With the shot that is fat, the ball goes a fraction of the distance you wanted it to go. If you hit the ball thin around the equator of the ball, your ball probably now rests on the next tee box.

The second whammy is that golfers know how hard it is to hit the ball. How often do we see the gorilla who hits the ball miles off the tee? Their shots look like something out of *Golf Digest*. But when they're standing over a twenty-yard chip shot, they are sweating bullets. Golf is a game of confidence. With tee shots and putts, I've seen some unconfident golfers hit some of the most beautiful shots in the world. Sometimes, you just get lucky. But when facing a difficult chip shot with very little confidence in your ability, it can be a recipe for disaster. Let me give you the best example I can. Tiger Woods is arguably the greatest golfer of all times. At minimum, he's one of the top two. But do you remember when Tiger Woods came back from his first forced exile? What is the shot that he struggled with the most? You got it. The chip shot.

We could go on and on about how difficult the wedge shot is. But I'm guessing that you already know that. So, let's get on to the solution. What is the best technique and mental approach to hitting a wedge shot?

Let's start by breaking the wedge shot down into the two main versions. The lob shot is a shot that is generally hit from twenty to fifty yards off the green. It tends to replicate more of a normal short iron shot. The shot is generally supposed to pop up quickly, achieve a reasonably high altitude, and come down softly on the green. Depending on your technique, some shots are designed to roll out to the flag. Other shots are designed to slam on brakes. The pros even have a third version that hits and backs up to the flag. If you're reading this book, you probably don't have that shot in your arsenal. So, if you can get to the point where you can hit a reliable shot of twenty to fifty yards that lands on and stays on the green, you will probably be a happy camper.

The other shot generally executed with a wedge is the chip shot. With the improvement of consistency of the grass around the green, more and more players are using their putters when they are off the green. Another club that is gaining in popularity, especially for high-handicap players, is the chipper. These are basically putters with more loft. The benefit is that they enable you to take a more comfortable and reliable putter swing. The added loft causes the shot to fly over the longer, more unpredictable grass and to settle onto the green where the ball rolls up to the pin like a putt. If you haven't experimented with a chipper, I would encourage you to check them out.

Some players chip with a longer iron, with the six iron being very popular. Another technique that helps with these longer irons is to stand the club up straight, like a putter. Raising the club up straight removes the heel of the club from the ground. Only the toe of the club touches the ground. That's less metal to come in contact with the ground, reducing your chances of hitting the chip fat. The benefit of hitting the upright six iron is that, like the chipper, you can hit the chip like a putt, skip over the bad stuff, and allow a more predictable roll up to the hole. Finally, some players like to chip with a fairway metal. The clubface is only slightly lofted, enabling you to hit it more like a putter, but, like the chipper, the loft causes the ball to fly over the bad stuff before settling down and rolling like a putt. And the larger, heavier clubhead is easier to slide through the grass behind the ball. It doesn't twist and turn like some lighter clubs can do. You will want to experiment with all these options before deciding which club is best for you to use for your chips.

But let's go back to the two basic wedge shots and talk technique. Let's start with the lob shot. When it comes to hitting a lob shot, my general observation is that golfers tend to hit the ball fat more than they hit it thin. Brand-new golfers are just the opposite. My general observation is that new golfers tend to be afraid to hit into the ground. Maybe it stems from a lecture they got as a kid when they dug a hole in the front yard. Maybe they're concerned that they'll break an arm or sprain a wrist if they hit into the terra firma. But for whatever reason, new golfers tend to top the ball on all shots more than they hit it fat.

Generally, that doesn't last too long. They quickly learned that no one is going to yell at them about taking a toupee. Or at least they won't if they replace their divot or add some sand to the divot scar. They also learn that they can hit the ball with the descending blow, take a three- to five-inch divot, and emerge unscathed. Once they get over that hurdle, they get to the point where their lob shots tend to be hit fat more often than they are thin.

Why is that? It's a basic issue of technique. How often do you see a golfer (including yourself) who hits the perfect lob shot during their practice swing? The tempo is wonderful. The legs slide easily through the backswing and the downswing. The club skims magically across the grass, sending little flecks of grass into the air. But when they step up over the ball, something happens. That fear and lack of confidence kicks in. The first thing that you will notice is that their tempo speeds up. A lot. Instead of that nice smooth, graceful swing, they swing as if they must get off the golf course quickly for an early date.

Secondly, and most damaging, they tend to drop their back shoulder when they come back through. Despite the significant loft of the wedge, golfers feel like they need to help the ball gain altitude. They drop the back shoulder in an effort to scoop the club under the ball and fling it into the air.

Thirdly, instead of bracing on their back foot, they allow their body to slide backward. Allowing your body to move backward in the downswing is okay. Watch a baseball player swinging at the ball, and you will see that their body goes backward first. But before the baseball player hits the ball, what do they do? They shift their weight forward. For maximum power, they are moving forward when they make contact with the ball. The same power-generating effect can help you hit your ball farther.

But for the golfer, the reason for moving your body forward is for another reason. You are moving your center of gravity forward. Your club head is going to come down and contact the ground at the middle of your body. If your body moves backward and doesn't move forward to regain your starting position, then your club is going to contact the ground behind the ball. It's just physics. You can't change it. So, the first key to making good contact with the ball when you hit a lob shot is to ensure that your body is centered over the ball when the clubface makes contact with the ball. Therefore, if you naturally sway back during your backswing, you must make sure that your body is moving forward when you make contact with the ball.

Do you not want to take a chance on swaying too far back on your backswing? Possibly going so far back that it's tough to get back to your original position? Then, what you need to do is to brace yourself on the inside of your back foot. When you take the club back, feel the pressure on the inside of your back foot. If you allow the pressure to transfer to the outside of your back foot, it allows your foot to roll back and your upper body sways backward. Here's a great drill to instill this feeling in your feet. Take one of your clubs and place it under your back shoe on the outside edge. With the club pushing back against the side of your foot, it directs your weight to transfer to the inside of your back foot. Feel that sensation. Obviously, you can't hit a shot out on the course with your least favorite club tucked under your shoe. But once you ingrain the feeling of your weight being on the inside of your back foot, you can transfer that feeling out onto the course.

On the range, place a club or alignment tool under the outside of your rear leg. Ingrain the feeling of loading up your weight on the inside of your back foot to prevent the sway.

Next, let's look at a natural stance designed to keep you from hitting behind the ball. When you set up over the lob shot, make your stance compact. Your feet should be no farther apart than your shoulders. In fact, the closer you keep your feet together, the more control you will have. You are striving for a nice, compact, and controlled shot. For lob shots, some people have their feet running parallel to each other and facing the front. Others find that it helps them to have a slightly open stance with their front foot turned out toward the target. Try both stances and just go with what feels the most comfortable and which stance delivers the most consistent control.

Now, the piece de resistance. Lean your body slightly forward and put more weight on your front foot. How much? You need to experiment. At least 60 percent of your weight. But, maybe as high as 70 percent of your weight. But be careful. If you put too much weight on your front foot, you might begin to feel off-balance. Or if you put too much weight on your front foot, your leg might begin to tremble. Put your weight on your front foot, but make sure you feel comfortable and in balance. By placing your weight on your front foot, you shift your center of balance slightly forward. This causes your club head to be slightly descending when it makes contact with the ball, with the swing bottoming out in front of the ball and after you have made contact with the ball.

The next thing we have to address is your tempo and speed. As I said earlier, the main difference between the practice swing and the actual swing is generally the speed with which you swing. There are basically three benefits of swinging fast. First, is if your natural rhythm is to do things quickly. All pros and good amateurs swing quickly on their downswing. But watch the speed of their backswings. It varies by player. Nick Price was known for his very fast backswing. When asked about it, he said that the fast swing was just his natural swing speed. If he tried to slow it down, he tended to be uncomfortable. His natural swing speed was fast.

But then look at the swing of Ernie Els or Fred Couples. Ernie isn't known as "The Big Easy" for no reason. He has a slow and graceful backswing. As for Fred Couples, you can time his backswing with a sun dial. But if you compare the speed with which they hit the ball, they are very similar. That's true for all pros. They hit the ball very hard with a fast and accelerating downswing. But, the speed with which they take the club back varies greatly by player. If your natural inclination is to swing quickly, do so, as long as you are making great contact with the ball. Remember, Nick, Ernie, Fred, and the other pros all have great hand-eye coordination. You don't, or you wouldn't be reading this book! So, even if you do everything else quickly, if you are having trouble finding that narrow window between the ball and the ground, try slowing down your backswing.

The next reason why people swing quickly is if they feel like they are losing control. That might sound contradictory. We just said you should slow down your backswing in order to gain more control. But now, I'm saying that swinging too slowly can cause you to lose control. Here's the problem. Any time you do something slowly, you are allowing time for bad things to creep in. This is especially true for wedge shots. Hitting that narrow window of opportunity requires intense concentration and focus. You would think that we should all be able to focus on something for at least three seconds. But, in the nervous world of golfing, it's tough to do. Sometimes, taking too long to complete the shot allows our mental focus to stray. Let's face it. The longer it takes you to complete something, the more opportunity you have for useless mental thoughts and doubts to creep in.

In addition to your mental focus, your physical performance can break down if you take too long to complete the shot. Things like involuntary muscle movement (or just good old-fashioned jerks) can creep in. The experts who do all the research suggest that the optimal relationship between the time taken for the backswing and the time taken for the downswing is a ratio of 3:1. Some people benefit by using a slower backswing with a ratio of 4:1. But the researchers have found that, as the golfer approaches a ratio of 5:1, bad things start to happen. So, if you find that your efforts to slow down the backswing are producing diminishing returns, such as a loss of mental or physical control, then use experimentation to find the optimal speed and tempo.

Finally, the third reason to swing quickly is to hit the ball hard and fast. But this one is a no-brainer. The lob shot is a control shot, not a distance shot. You don't want to crush the ball when you are only thirty yards from the flag! Therefore, the main reason to swing quickly is negated.

Bottom line, unless dictated by your natural body rhythm or you find you lose control when you slow down too much, the best thing you can do to improve your lob shots is slow down and smell the roses. But, in the heat of battle, that's easier said than done. The main tip that I can give you is to force yourself to swing in slow motion. Right before you hit the ball, tell yourself to swing in slow motion. That's tough to do from the fairway because we tend to feel like we have to hit the ball hard (and the brain translates that to swinging quickly) or our shot will come up short. But you only have about thirty feet to the flag! Simply tell yourself to swing in slow motion. You'll speed up. People naturally do. The result will be a nice, graceful swing, making good contact with the ball.

Besides shifting your weight back and not being able to shift it back forward to its original starting point (or actually a little bit ahead of it, as you want to be driving the clubhead under the ball and forward), there is another thing that can cause you to hit the ball fat or thin. This is the length of your arm and where it returns to as you begin your downswing. When you set up to hit your shot, the ball is a certain distance from your shoulder. If you had a third arm and a tape measurer, you could measure the actual distance.

If, when you swing the club back or when you begin your downswing, your arm is stretched out or contracted, the point on the ball where you make contact changes. Let's take the more common scenario. When you pull the club back, in your nervousness or anxiousness to hit the ball, you speed up your swing or swing more aggressively. What does the centrifugal force do? It naturally causes the arm to extend farther and straighter out from the body. If your arm extends out just a half of an inch farther than the original distance, what happens? You contact the ball (or the ground, as the case may be) a half of an inch farther down than the optimal contact point. Conversely, if, in your nervousness, you bend your arm a little bit, or otherwise reduce the length of your arm by a half an inch, what happens? Correct. You make contact with the ball a half an inch farther up, or just about the equator of the ball. Then you watch as it flies over the green.

So, how do you guarantee that the length of your arm always remains the same? Well, of course. As we discussed earlier, you form a pendulum. Remember the pendulum from your high school science class? Because a pendulum is anchored to something, unless you use cheap rope that stretches, the ball at the end of the pendulum always stays the same distance from the anchor. That's the effect that you want to create.

But how do you do that? Simple, you have to anchor your arm to your body. But wait. Isn't that illegal? Only anchoring your putter to your chest. For any other shot, you can anchor your elbow to your body. Think about this for a second. Why were long putters that could be anchored to your chest invented? Because they were able to create a pendulum effect. The putting stroke became more consistent and reliable because of the pendulum effect. Now, of course, we don't want to allow something that made the game easier to be allowed, so anchoring was made illegal for putting. But the powers that be haven't gotten around to outlawing it for pitching and chipping. So, let's take advantage of this technique to improve the quality of our wedge play!

Here's another way to look at it. What is the most utilized drill in golf? I've never seen a survey on that one. But from general observation, I would say that it's the drill to tuck a towel or golf glove under your armpit. And sometimes under both armpits. Why do you do that? Well, it goes back to the advice for virtually every iron or wood/metal shot to keep your rear elbow tucked into your side. If your elbow disconnects from your side, the towel or glove falls out of your armpit. That makes it pretty easy to see that your arm became disconnected. If the towel or glove remains in place, you will hit a better shot.

So, why do you want to keep your elbow connected to your midsection? The pendulum effect. If your elbow disconnects from your body, your arm tends to move up and out. If it's really far away from your side, you get the famous "chicken wing." But even a small separation can cause your arm to get up and away from you. When you bring the club back down across the ball from out to in, it probably leads to a slice. But, even if it doesn't, moving the club away from the body a half inch in either direction can cause you to hit the ball up to a half inch on either side of the sweet spot. Hence, the popular armpit drill to ensure that you are using a good pendulum effect to return the clubface to where it started. Again, if it works for the rest of your irons, it's destined to help you make good contact with the club that requires the most precise contact with the ball.

Okay. Got it. Pendulum effect. But how do you pull it off? It's actually quite simple. Before you initiate your backswing, feel the elbow of your rear arm tucked firmly against your side. Then, as you pull back the club, make sure that it stays there. It will be a bit awkward at first. But you will get used to it. If you take a really large backswing, you have to disconnect your elbow in order to stretch out the club. But, with a twenty- to forty-yard pitch, you don't need to take a long backswing. Hit the driving range with a bucket of balls and work on just keeping your elbow close to your side as you hit pitch after pitch shot. You will be amazed at how much more consistent your contact and your distance will become.

Next, let's look at the other shot commonly hit with the wedge, the chip shot. The first tip for hitting a good chip shot is the same one we learned for the lob shot. Keep the elbow anchored to your side to maximize your pendulum effect. One good thing is that the shorter backswing of the chip shot will make it easier to keep your elbow anchored to your side.

The next technique for making solid contact at the base of the ball in your chip shot is going to surprise you. Your first reaction will probably be that it doesn't make sense. But hear me out. In setting up for your chip, you actually want to move the ball forward in your stance. Instead of having the ball in front of your back foot, you want the ball directly across from the heel or instep of your front foot. Now, here's what you are probably thinking regarding why that can't work. If your problem is that you tend to chunk the ground behind the ball, doesn't placing the ball forward in your stance open your shot up to a whole lot more of that nasty grass? Yes, except you are going to make one other adjustment to your swing. What tends to cause you to hit behind the ball (or in the belly of the ball) is that you are making a steep, descending swing. The problem with a steep descending swing is that it reduces your margin of error. When you bring the clubface down, it makes contact with the ball, the ground, or thin air at one spot.

Instead, what you want is a more sweeping technique. It gives you more margin for error. Yes, the edge of your club still has to make contact at the base of the ball or in the grass slightly below the ball (assuming that you aren't hitting off hard pan or dead grass). But a sweeping motion doesn't impact one specific spot on the ground. Instead, it sweeps over the grass. Think of the difference between a B-17 bomber and a Stuka dive bomber. If the plane becomes inoperative, the Stuka bomber continues diving straight into the ground. But the B-17 glides down to a perfect three-point landing. Or at least, that's the theory!

So, if you want to avoid a chip shot with a steep, descending blow, you don't want to set up for the shot with a stance that encourages a steep, descending blow. You want a stance that encourages a low, sweeping swing. Placing your ball forward in your stance encourages this shot. As most of the alternative techniques in this book do, this one will require some practice. But set up with your weight leaning forward, the ball off your front foot, and your elbow anchored to your midsection. Then take a nice, sweeping backswing and then swing through the ball.

Here's another tip to make solid contact with the ball on your chip shots. Instead of keeping your wrists firm and swinging the clubface back as far as you need to in order to hit the ball the required distance, allow your wrists to hinge on the backswing. Here's why this is important. If your mission is simply to make solid contact with the golf ball, are you more likely to do this by bringing the club head back six inches or sixteen inches? The obvious answer is that the shorter the swing, the better your odds are for making solid contact. It's quite simple, actually. The farther you bring the clubface back from the ball, the greater the chance of the clubface getting out of line with where you wanted to return to.

So, if the clubface needs to come back sixteen inches in order to have the correct speed and mass to propel the ball the right distance, you have two choices. First, you can keep your wrists firm and swing the clubface back sixteen inches. Second, you can swing your hands back six inches, but allow the wrists to hinge, so that the club head moves back sixteen inches from the ball. What is the benefit of this maneuver? Well first, we have already determined that there is less that can go wrong if your hands are only swinging back six inches, as opposed to swinging back sixteen inches.

Secondly, you can't let your wrists hinge if you are squeezing the club for dear life. It's an age-old conclusion that tension is the enemy of a good golf swing. Because of people's lack of confidence in their wedge play, you are most likely to be tense during a chip shot. The tension in the muscles in your arm prevents you from being able to swing the club in a free-flowing manner. In addition, the tension encourages you to swing rapidly, in order to get the shot over as quickly as possible. Both of these are problems when it comes to hitting a good chip shot. But, in order to allow the wrist to hinge, we have to reduce the tension in our arms and grip. Even if this benefit is only psychological (and we know it will have a positive physical effect), the value of swinging with a loose

For the best wedge shots, hit the ball forward in your stance. Notice that the weight is on your front foot. The anchor point for your pendulum is right above the ball. The wrists are hinged to provide more power but with less loss of control from a big swing.

grip is immeasurable. It simply leads to a more confident and tension-free swing.

But there's even one more additional benefit of this technique. Remember the pendulum effect? By anchoring the elbow of your back arm against your midsection, you are able to keep the distance from your elbow down to your clubhead a constant distance. Well, the hinging of your wrist on the chip shot creates a second pendulum effect. When you bring the clubface back sixteen inches with very stiff wrists, the distance that your arms are extended can vary, especially, if the stiffness of your wrists is leading to tension in your arms, or it encourages you to swing too quickly. But when you break your wrists, you have formed a second pendulum. You have added another ten inches to your backswing, but the distance between your wrists and the end of the club remains constant. Just like a pendulum.

The next time you set up over a delicate chip shot, take a few practice swings. Amateur golfers are sometimes reluctant to take multiple practice swings. They feel self-conscious that everyone is watching and waiting on them. But watch how the pros approach a delicate chip shot. They never hit the shot without a practice swing. Rarely do they take just one practice swing. If they're chipping from taller grass off the edge of the green, they are using their practice swing to measure the resistance of the grass. In addition, they are ingraining the muscle memory in their arms so that they can immediately step up and repeat that same free-flowing, confident swing. Your game will benefit from multiple practice swings.

Here's one final tip on making good contact with the ball. When I first developed these techniques, I found that I still had a tendency to hit my chips fat or thin. Why? I had convinced myself that my use of physics and mechanics had created the perfect swing. I found myself assuming that the technique was infallible, and so, I could just swing the club without having to concentrate and focus on making solid contact with the ball. It was a disaster. The natural tendency of a bad golfer is to simply swing the club generally as quickly as possible. Why? Because we just want to get it over with! We know that by sheer, dumb luck, we hit about every third shot well. Well, at least decently. So, we swing as quickly as possible with no focus on what we are doing, in order to get through the inevitable as rapidly as possible and in the hope that the shot will be a good one.

Instead, realize that the mechanical technique that I have provided will merely increase the odds of you making solid contact with the ball. It won't guarantee that you make solid contact with the ball. There are still too many things that can go wrong. Once you master the techniques, you will still need to focus your eyes on the spot where you want to make contact with the ball. Minimize your swing thoughts. One or two swing thoughts are the max. Anything beyond that is going to clutter up your mind, rob you of focus, and mess up your shot. Go through your technique as a PRE-SHOT routine. Once you have the stance correct, the weight on your front foot, the ball forward in your stance, and the proper grip on the ball, forget about your technique. Focus your eyes on where you want to make contact with the ball and let that be the only thing that you concentrate on as you take the swing. The combination of correct technique and proper focus is what will improve your chips.

Which brings us to our next technique. Even after you master a consistent technique of anchoring our elbow and moving our body forward through the ball, if we pull back the club the same distance, it's always going to go the same distance. And we never seem to have exactly the same chip twice. So, what is a good reliable technique to regulate the distance that we chip?

This one may surprise you. Remember how we talked about how pros with great hand-eye coordination don't want you to get too mechanical? They want you to hit everything by feel? Well, this is one shot when they encourage amateurs to be mechanical. Feel techniques are great for shots where you just swing away. The length of your drive can vary by as much as fifty yards (even more if you really duff that drive). Who cares? Just measure the remaining yardage, pick an appropriate club, and whale away.

But every pro knows that that much inconsistency in distance doesn't work in a chip shot. So, even they rely on some mechanical techniques. And the most popular is the clock face. Virtually every golf school has a device that replicates a clock face. It's usually a large plywood sheet, turned at the optimal swing plane for a lob, pitch, or chip shot with a hole in it. You stick your body through the hole until the plywood board is at roughly your waist level. The first thing you learn is to swing the club back parallel and as closely as possible as you can to the face of the clock on the plywood board. In his famous instructional books, Ben Hogan encouraged his readers to visualize it as a glass plane. If you swung too close or too far away from the plane of glass, you would crack it with your arms or the club. They can't use a glass plane on the teaching range. It's way too messy. So, they settle for the plywood board.

Once you master the correct swing plane, then the pro calls your attention to the clock face drawn on the plywood. Your head is at 12:00. In your stance, your club is at roughly 6:00. The pro instructs you to swing the club back to 7:00. And you note how far you hit the pitch. Next, you swing the club back to 8:00, and you note how far you hit the ball. Then comes a swing back to 9:00. And so forth. You can even refine your distance even farther. Note how much you bend your wrists. You can swing the club back to 9:00 with the club pointed straight out. Or you can allow your wrists to cock. The centrifugal force, or as it is known in the golf swing, the "lag," can add a bit farther distance to your shot. And finally, the amount of drive in your legs will affect your distance. You can hit a pitch shot with just your upper body. But if you allow your lower body to go back and through the shot, your ball will go farther.

Imagining the clock face, my hands are at 7:00

How do you master this clock technique? It's time to hit the range. First, experiment with just hitting balls from 7:00, 8:00, and 9:00. Then, experiment with your wrist cock. Then, add in a little lower leg movement. Memorize how far you pitch the ball with each combination. Then, practice, practice, practice. Ingrain in your memory exactly what shot to hit based on the distance you want the ball to roll (and don't forget that balls tend to roll faster on a closely mowed green than they do on a gnarly driving range). When you get over the ball, just envision the face of the clock. Take a practice swing. And make sure you are replicating the swing for that distance that you honed out on the range. Not only will your odds of the ball

Now my hands are at 8:00. Make a mental note of how much farther your shot goes with this swing.

going the right distance be enhanced, but the confidence of knowing that you can hit that shot helps give you a consistent, reliable pitch shot.

Note that, although my hands are at 9:00, the hinging of my wrists are creating a wider arc and generating more power from a minimal amount of backswing. That helps you keep control of the club.

My final two technique suggestions for hitting short chip shots are ones that I have not included in my universal list of techniques. Instead, I listed them here at the end of the section as simply a "disaster avoidance" technique. Pull these out of the bag only if, despite the other suggestions that I have given you, you are in the midst of an important round with big money on the line, and you still find yourself hitting the ball fat. Your arms are screaming at you because you have chunked so many shots. If that's the case, try these final techniques.

First, when you set up over the ball, move your focus about an inch in front of the ball (closer to the hole). Simply imagine that you want your swing to shallow out about an inch in front of the ball. You would think that this technique would cause you to hit the ball thin. But remember, this is a solution to be used only when your body is just not cooperating and you are hitting everything about an inch behind the ball. If you focus your attention in front of the ball and attempt to shallow out your swing approximately one inch in front of the ball, then you miraculously make contact with the ball at its base where you wanted to make contact. Again, pros would laugh at this suggestion. But newsflash, you're not a professional golfer. When your hand-eye coordination isn't working, it isn't working. And you have to take radical solutions. This is one of those radical solutions. File it away, and only use it if absolutely necessary.

It's the same thing for this second suggestion. This technique is only to be used in times of emergency. I have recommended hitting your chips with the ball forward in your stance. This allows the club to skim across the grass before going under the ball, thus avoiding the descending chip shot that hits fat or thin if it doesn't descend at the right spot. But this final emergency technique should be used if you find that you just can't get the sweeping technique to make contact at the right spot. You are still thudding the wedge behind the ball or on the equator of the ball.

First, move the ball back in your stance. Place it across from the toe of your trail foot. Now, lean forward so that your center of gravity is solidly on your front foot. Don't lean too far forward that you feel tension in your lower body. At max, place 60 percent or 70 percent of your weight on your front foot. Place the face of the wedge behind the ball. Now, very importantly, raise the lead edge of the wedge to about a half of an inch up on the back of the ball. In other words, hover the clubface above the ground, not starting flat on the ground.

Why is this important? Because with this descending shot, I can guarantee that 90 percent of the time, you will hit

If you just can't make good contact with the wedge with the ball up front in your stance, move it to the back. Make sure your weight is forward and your hands are ahead of the ball. Then, hover the club face at the center of the ball as you are most likely to hit the ball fat than thin with this shot.

the ball fat, rather than thin. Under pressure, your natural inclination is to lean forward and extend your arms. In their intensity to hit the ball, most high-handicap golfers tend to lean into the shot. Very few pull away from the ball, hitting it thin. If you are among the few that do this, then don't hover the club. But, for most golfers, hovering the club gives you a little more margin for error to prevent you from plowing a trough behind the ball.

When you take your swing, bring the clubface back slowly and with intense concentration. Remember, this is not a power shot. This is a control shot. Even if the slow swing results in you only hitting the chip halfway to the hole, because you started the shot just off the green, the result is that you are now putting the ball. A speedy, out-of-control shot that hits the ball fat or thin results in the ball coming up short of the green or on the far side of the green. Nothing is more frustrating than hitting a chip shot, only to have to hit it again.

There is one more visual image that can help you with this shot. Don't think that you are hitting a golf shot. Think that you are simply "nudging" the ball onto the green. Even with a slow backswing and controlled forward swing, let the loft of the club, the mass of the clubhead and the natural inertia built up in the downswing nudge the ball onto the green. Frankly, you will be surprised how far the ball will roll. Remember, the pros are hitting the ball with downward force that puts backspin on the ball. This backspin controls the length that the ball rolls. That's how pros control the distance their ball rolls. They are good enough to be able to control how much they spin the ball. But you don't have that skill. You aren't putting a lot of spin on the ball. So, take advantage of that. Don't try to put backspin on the ball. Nudge it onto the green and then let the ball roll out closer to the hole. A good chip and a two putt generally result in bogies. That's far better than the scores that come from hitting your chip shot fat or thin.

THE SHORT IRONS

Why do they call them short irons? Because we generally hit them short of where we want to! Or farther than we want them to go. But rarely the distance that we want them to go. But with some simple fixes, you can begin to hit your short irons with greater accuracy and dependability.

You'll notice that I use the word accuracy. For the high-handicap golfer, the word accuracy and long irons, fairway metals, or driver are rarely mentioned in the same sentence. With the driver and the fairway metals, our objective is generally to advance the ball down the fairway, trying to keep it in the short grass. With the long irons, accuracy is a plus. But for most of us, simply getting our shots of 150 yards or more somewhere close to the green would be a big improvement.

However, with the short irons, accuracy is a must. While most people understand this, they rarely use this knowledge to differentiate their technique for hitting short irons from their technique for the longer clubs. So, the first lesson of hitting short irons is to realize that trying to hit the club as hard as you can is the biggest mistake that you will make. When you are trying to hit the ball only one hundred yards, you don't need to swing as hard as you can in order to get it there. If a more deliberate, controlled swing is causing you to come up short, simply use a longer club!

Feeling peer pressure and using a particular club just because your more athletically gifted golf partner uses that club for a certain distance is the number one reason that they are on the green and you aren't. Heck, they don't have to know what club you are using. In fact, it's a violation of the rules of golf for them to ask what club you are using. Ditch the ego and use the club that you need to get the ball to the green with a smooth, deliberate swing.

The stances for short irons, long irons, fairway metals, and the driver are all similar, with three exceptions. In your stance, assume the athletic position discussed in the chapter on the stance. But most golfers do find that a little more knee bend is beneficial for the short irons than for the longer clubs. This is because the short irons are shorter. Also, you are going to use the most descending blow, and high-handicap golfers find it easier to come down on the ball and take a divot if they have a little bit more bend to their knees and are closer to the ball.

The second difference is the width of your stance. The general rule of thumb is that the shorter the club, the closer together you keep your feet. For the short irons, I would recommend drawing an imaginary line down from the outside of your shoulders. Try to keep the width of your stance within those imaginary lines. As you go to longer clubs, you will find that widening your stance will give you a bit more power, as required by those longer clubs.

The final difference would be the placement of the ball. Generally speaking, for short iron shots, you will place the ball in the middle of your stance. The ball will be a little farther forward for your long irons. It will be almost to the heel of your front foot for the fairway woods. And you'll generally tee up the ball off your front foot for the driver.

However, even though the conventional wisdom is to align the ball in the middle of your stance for the short irons, don't assume this is always the case for you. Remember, that's where the pros put it, and they can do things that you can't do. With the short irons, your objective is to hit the ball with a descending blow. This means that the ball should be where the front edge of your clubface makes contact with the ground in your natural swing. Your natural swing may not be the same as that of the pro. This is the part where you head out to the driving range. Without a ball in front of you, take a natural descending blow swing. Use a tee to mark where your clubhead makes contact with the ground. That's where you want your ball to be.

But one word of caution. Take lots of swings and place lots of tees before you determine your natural descending point. You don't want the point to be where you "try" to hit the ball. As you know, your odds of replicating that performance on a regular basis aren't good. You want the point where you place the ball to be at your "natural" point of a descending blow shot. In your normal swing, your odds of delivering that shot over and over again are greater.

You will find that you may need to make an adjustment to your normal ball alignment. If you find during a round of golf that, for whatever reason, you are hitting your short irons fat (into the ground behind the ball), go ahead and set up your stance with your ball slightly farther back in your stance. I know that sounds like a "Band-Aid" remedy. It is. You don't have time to fix your swing during a round of golf. So, it is sometimes necessary to throw in a Band-Aid or two to simply get you through the round. This is one of those occasions.

Here's a technique that can greatly enhance your short iron play. Although this technique might be reserved until your golf skills have become more prolific, it's a good thing to keep in the back of your mind. If you want to get a bit higher loft out of your irons, but still get a similar distance traveled, a good technique is to move the ball a slight bit forward in your stance. Let's say that you deviated a bit from the beaten path, and you find a tall tree between you and the green. You might need to use this technique. First, be realistic. Does your normal shot with that short iron give you enough height to clear the tree? If the answer is no, don't be a hero. Use a long iron to punch out under the tree to the fairway.

But if you have that shot in your arsenal, you can enhance your odds of getting enough height to clear the tree by moving the ball up a bit in your stance. What you're doing when you move the ball forward in your stance is adding loft to the club. This added loft might make the difference in clearing the tree. This technique is thoroughly covered in most instructional books and videos, so I'm not going to spend a whole lot of time on it. I simply wanted to make the point that where your ball is in your stance for a short iron shot is not always a given.

Once you've taken your stance, the number one thing to remember for a successful short iron shot is the importance of bracing your backswing on the inside of your trailing foot. In this book, we've spoken numerous times on the importance of the pendulum motion and having a constant anchor for your pendulum motion. The principles behind a pendulum are the most important element of having a consistent repeating swing. The height of Iron Byron doesn't change from swing to swing. Iron Byron doesn't sway backward or forward as it takes a swing. The secret of the consistency of Iron Byron is that it establishes a pendulum that swings back and through the ball in the same manner with every swing. That's what you have to achieve to successfully hit a short iron, or for that matter, any golf club.

In taking a swing of the short iron, one of the most common problems is that the golfer tends to sway backward as they take their backswing. If you look at slow-motion footage of some of the best golfers in the world, they do sway slightly back in their downswing. But here's the thing. They are athletic and coordinated enough to be able to swing back to their original starting position when they make contact with the ball.

Watch athletes in virtually any other sport where they need to generate power. Look at the baseball player as they hit the ball. Watch the tennis pro as they hit a forehand. They will sway backward, but then move forward, as they make contact with the ball. Some of the best golfers in the world do that also. But you're not one of the best golfers in the world. If you sway back, your odds of moving forward back to your original starting position with forward momentum are slim. So, you simply have to accept the fact that you're not going to hit your pitching wedge 150 yards. But remember our first principle of swinging a short iron. Your goal is accuracy, not power. Even though you don't generate the power to hit a pitching wedge 150 yards, if you can hit a six iron 150 yards, you're in good shape.

Bracing your backswing on your inside back foot prevents your body from swaying back. It is relatively easy to do. Take a practice swing. Feel your weight on the front side of your back or trail foot. If you feel the weight on the backside or outside of your rear foot, this means that your weight has shifted too far to the back of your stance. Earlier in the book, I provided you with an excellent technique to give you the feel of placing your weight on the inside of your back foot. Take one of your clubs, an alignment rod or some other similar object and place it under the backside of your back foot. Now take a practice swing. The club or other tool will force your weight onto the front side of your trailing foot. Feel that sensation. Then remove the tool (because remember, you can't place it there during your real swing) and feel that sensation with your natural swing.

Now, you are ready to begin the backswing. With your short iron, you will probably have your slowest takeaway from the ball. Why? First, power is not critical in the shot. Remember, our goal is accuracy. While virtually all high-handicap amateur golfers swing way too quickly, this is one shot where you don't need speed in order to generate power. Second, since accuracy is so important, it is critical to hit your short iron shots in the sweet spot at the center of the club. You can get by with the mishit on a driver or iron. Sure, that means you won't hit those shots down the middle of the fairway. But you can still advance a long iron shot, fairway metal shot, or driver down the fairway, even if you don't catch it precisely on the screws. But with the short iron shot, making contact with the center of the clubface is critical. Therefore, focus on the ball, slow down, take a very deliberate backswing with a consistent rhythm and tempo, and make solid contact with the ball.

One of the biggest mistakes that most high-handicap golfers make is to overswing on their short irons. Why would someone think that they have to take the club way back in order to hit a shot? In order to generate power. But let's go back to the first principle of hitting a short iron. Your objective is not to generate power. It is to hit an accurate shot. The farther back you take the club, the more you decrease your odds of making solid contact with the ball.

My advice is to visualize your short iron shot as having an L-shaped look. Imagine your body as the face of a clock. Your head would be at 12:00 and your clubface addressing the ball is at 6:00. Now, picture your arms going back to somewhere between 9:00 and 10:00. That's it. No farther. In the short iron shot, you want your wrists to hinge. So, visualize your arms swinging out to roughly 9:00 on the clubface with your wrists hinged to a ninety-degree angle. This is the L-shaped backswing that you want to achieve.

I know what you're thinking. "If I only swing back that far, I'm not going to be able to hit a very powerful shot." First, go back and read the first paragraph in this chapter. Your objective is not power. Your objective is accuracy. If this technique, which is designed to maximize the accuracy of your shot, is not generating enough distance, then use a higher club. Your objective is control, and the shorter your backswing, the greater control you will have in this shot.

But let me leave you with one other thought on the L-shaped backswing that tops out at 9:00 on the clock face. Your arms will not stop at 9:00! This is one of the weirdest things about golf. Every time I've had my swing videotaped, my arms and club always go back farther than I think they are going. It all started when I took a lesson, and the pro videotaped my swing. After watching my swing, the pro told me that I was going beyond parallel in the backswing with my driver. I told him that that could not be the case. The sensation at the top of my backswing was that my arms were above the level of my head and that the club was pointing down the line, parallel to the ground. He showed me the video of my swing. Much to my surprise, he was right. My club was beyond parallel, in a crude imitation of John Daly.

When he filmed my short iron shots, inevitably the video proved that my arms and club were going back farther than it felt like they were going. While this sensation may be unique to me, I don't think that's the case. Have someone videotape your short iron swing. Try to take your arms back to the 9:00 position. Then, watch it on the video. I'm betting that you will

Even through you feel like you are creating a L-shaped swing, the momentum of the clubhead and the bend in your wrists will result in the club going farther back. This will generate plenty of distance for a short shot.

see that your arms are actually going back to 10:00 or 11:00. But the mental image of your hands going back to 9:00, and very importantly, going back to the same position each time, will enable you to make a much more controlled and consistent contact with the ball.

Believe it or not, I can give you another technique where what you feel happening is probably, in fact, not occurring. This is the famous "pause at the top" technique. My advice is to pause at the top of your backswing. Frankly, this pause will help you, not only with the short irons, but with every club you swing. The reason that the pause is so beneficial is that it prevents you from swinging the club too quickly. One of the main errors that most high-handicap golfers make is that they swing too quickly. But simply swinging quickly isn't the problem. Golf pros swing really, really quickly. And they hit the ball really well.

But for you, the problem with swinging too quickly is that you don't allow the full backswing to occur. One of the most important factors in how you strike the ball and where it goes is where your club is at the back of the swing. Again, I'm not going to dwell too much on the position of the club at the back of the swing, because these principles are universal for both good and bad golfers. But let me just say that one of the most important principles is to swing the club back on plane and to make sure that the club is pointing to your target at the top of the backswing.

If you rush the transition between the backswing and the downswing, several bad things are going to happen. First, as we have already discussed, your club does not "set" in the optimal position at the top of the swing. Second, beginning the downswing before the backswing is completed is, most likely, going to resort in a jerking motion. Jerking motions in golf are bad. They tend to be accompanied by a tightening in the muscles of the arms. A jerky downswing tends to take your club offline, resulting in a swing that does not make solid contact in the sweet spot of the clubface.

Third, remember that your goal is accuracy. This means hitting your shot roughly the same distance each time. Your mental calculation of which club you hit is based on the average distance that you hit that club. The average distance you hit that club is based on how far back you bring the club in your downswing. But if you initiate your downswing before the club has gotten to its full arc and jerk your club down at an inconsistent speed, your distance is going to vary with every swing of the club.

Feeling the sensation of a pause at the top of your backswing means that your hands, arms, and the club have reached the same consistent spot where you want them to be at the top of your backswing. You will see some really good professional golfers who actually have a relatively lengthy pause at the top of their swing. But you are not one of these golfers. If you bring your club to a complete halt at the top of your backswing, my experience is that, psychologically, you will feel like you need to dramatically shift to the downswing in order to compensate for this loss in momentum. Ironically, golfers who pause too long at the top tend to then jerk down on their downswing with an adverse effect.

Another effect of the overextended pause is the fact that one of the biggest problems for high-handicap golfers is that they tend to lose their focus and concentration during the swing. You wouldn't think that focusing on something for a matter of mere seconds would be that hard. But if you're reading this book, you know that focusing on the ball is hard. The longer it takes you to swing the club, the more chance you have for negative thoughts, competing swing thoughts, and other factors to creep into your shot, destroying your focus on making solid contact with the ball.

So, what I'm recommending is to have the "sensation" of having a pause at the top. And this is where we get to my earlier statement that this is the second case where what you feel like you are doing, and what is happening, are not necessarily one and the same. Let's go back to the videotape. When videotaping my swing, I have this sensation that I am pausing at the top of my backswing. But when I reviewed the video, there is no pause. In reality, my swing in the video is a nice smooth transition from the backswing to the downswing. Mentally, I am sensing a pause at the top. But realistically, it is simply causing me to complete the backswing and then smoothly transition to the downswing. Practice the pause in front of the mirror and have someone videotape your swing. You'll see what I'm talking about.

What is the best way to initiate the downswing? For the longer clubs, I'm going to talk about how your downswing is initiated by the lower body. For those clubs, you begin the downswing by shifting your lower legs, knees, and hips toward the target. The hands simply follow along with this forward inertia. But that technique is designed to generate power. Power is not our goal with the short irons. So, the downswing with the short irons is initiated by the arms. The best advice I ever heard when initiating the short iron swing came from Hale Irwin. I had the pleasure of playing a round of golf at a corporate event with Hale Irwin not long after he had won his third U. S. Open. Prior to playing eighteen holes, Hale Irwin gave us some tips on the driving range.

His advice on hitting an accurate short iron shot is to feel as if you are pulling down on the cord of a church bell. When you get to the top of your backswing, and have felt that mental pause, pull down with your arms as if you are pulling down on a bell cord. This will create the sensation of pulling your arms down straight through the ball. After all, when you pull the church bell, you don't pull the cord from side to side. You pull the cord straight down. That's what you want in the shot to increase your accuracy.

The other benefit of having the sensation of pulling down on the bell cord is that this is the feel of the shot required to hit a descending blow. With the driver, you want to hit an ascending blow. You do not want your driver face to make contact with the grass. It reaches the bottom of the arc and is actually ascending before you make contact with the ball. With the fairway metals, you want to have more of a sweeping motion. As we will discuss in the chapter on fairway metals, some good golfers recommend taking a divot with your fairway metals. But most golfers suggest a sweeping motion where we make contact with the ball as we sweep across the grass.

But the iron shots require a more descending blow. Your objective is to make contact with the ball right before the clubface penetrates the grass. The clubface proceeds to plow through the grass, creating a divot on the front side of the ball. In order to hit a descending blow, your club needs to have more of a V-shaped motion than a U-shaped motion. The shorter backswing and the sensation of pulling down on the bell cord will enable you to have a more V-shaped swing and a descending blow on the ball.

*When you reach the top of our backswing with a short
iron, imagine you are pulling down on a bell cord. This
gives you an aggressive swing through the ball for greater
power and control. You can use a shorter backswing for
better control, but still get the distance that you need.*

Now you are ready to hit the short iron shot. I have given
you several techniques for hitting the shot. But do not, I repeat, do not think about these techniques when hitting the
ball. If you do, your brain will be so jumbled up that you will
never be able to focus on the ball and make solid contact. This
is the part where you go back and read the chapter on the pre-
shot routine. My best advice is to take a practice swing as you
stand behind the ball, not as you address the ball. Again, my
rationale is that your muscle memory will last long enough to

get you through the shot. Taking your practice swing behind the ball enables you to immediately take your stance over the ball, increasing your odds of getting lined up correctly with the spot that you have chosen, on the line between your ball and the hole.

It is during this practice swing behind the ball that you are thinking about the width of your feet, where the ball is in your stance, that you have your elbow in tightly against your trailing side, that you are taking a slow deliberate backswing up to the L shape at 9:00, that you are taking a mental pause at the top, and that you are pulling down on the bell cord as you swing the club in a descending blow down through the ball and into the earth. Let me repeat. If you try to think of all that in your actual shot, you will mess it up. So, use your practice swing behind the ball to ingrain in your muscles the technique that you want to use. If you find that that's too many things to think about in your practice swing, take more than one practice swing. Don't worry that you are playing too slowly. A practice swing takes about a second.

In fact, here's a technique to get in the number of swings you need to incorporate all of your swing thoughts without holding up everyone. If your partner is "out," or the farthest from the hole, they are going to swing first. But if you are far enough away from them, you can quietly review your swing thoughts and take one or more practice swings while they are taking their shot. Just make sure you are not in their peripheral vision or make any noise that could distract them. That way, you get your practice swings out of the way and you are ready to address your ball the moment your partner finishes their shot.

Then stride confidently up to the ball. Focus on aligning your stance so that you are hitting in the direction you want to go. Do not mess with your grip at this point. Remember, your grip should be the first thing that you take before you began your practice swing behind the ball. If you mess with your grip at this point, it's only a distraction, and is likely to make you forget where you're trying to hit the ball.

Right before you hit the ball, you want to take your waggle. But remember, it's okay to use your waggle to take a last-minute practice backswing. You are not going to practice your downswing, because that would result in your making contact with the ball. Simply use your waggle as an opportunity to swing the club back slowly and deliberately to your L-shaped location and pause. Bring the clubface back down behind the ball and focus on the ball. When I say focus, I mean focus. Forget everything else that is around you. Forget where your partners are. Forget what the weather is doing. Blank out everything around you.

If you want to see how this is done, watch the movie *The Legend of Bagger Vance*. Watch the scene where Bagger Vance describes to Matt Damon's character how Bobby Jones blocks out everything else around him as he places his total focus on making solid contact with the ball. Some golfers find it beneficial to focus on a spot at the back of the ball. Some golfers who have a tendency to hit the ball fat actually focus on a spot on the front of the ball. Just do whatever works for you. The important point is to place your entire mental focus on making solid contact with the ball. The muscle memory that you gained from that final practice swing will provide the direction to your muscles as they simply replicate the swing that you just did. So, blot the L-shaped swing, the 9:00 on the clock face, and the pause at the top completely out of your mind. Totally focus on the ball.

THE LONG IRONS

Much of the technique in hitting the long irons is similar to the short irons. So, I'm only going to focus on some of the key differences associated with hitting a long iron. First, the main difference between a short iron and a long iron is that the long iron requires more of a sweeping swing than the descending blow utilized with the short iron. Now, don't read into that sentence that we don't want to have a descending blow with the long iron shot. All iron shots require a descending blow. One of the biggest mistakes that high-handicap golfers make is that they feel like, because the long irons have less loft, that they have to help the ball get up in the air. That's not the way it works.

I wish I could explain why this happens, but it's physics, and I slept through physics class. Not that my physics professor spent a whole lot of time on the physics of the golf shot. If they had, maybe I would've paid more attention to the class. And come to think of it, maybe they did, but I slept through the whole thing. The bottom line, though, is that the physics of the situation means that hitting down on a golf ball makes it go higher in the air. Go figure.

The second difference between hitting a short iron and hitting a long iron is in our setup. As mentioned in our chapter on stance, while the ball is normally positioned in the middle of your stance for a short iron shot, it should be a little bit farther forward in our stance for a long iron shot.

The next difference in our setup is that most golfers will benefit by having the clubface on a long iron shot slightly open. For your short iron and wedge shots, the face of your club should be totally neutral. Your job during the swing is to return the clubface back to this neutral position, perpendicular to your body so that the ball comes straight off the clubface. Obviously, you may find it necessary to deviate from this rule of thumb. For example, if you needed to fade an iron shot around the tree, you would need to open the clubface, open your stance, hit the ball to the left of the tree, and let it curl back around the tree. If you needed to draw the ball around the tree, you would do the opposite. You would need to close the clubface, close your stance (with your lead foot slightly ahead of your trail foot), start the ball to the right, and curl it back to the left. But we're just talking about your normal setup. For the short irons, you want your clubface to be neutral in its alignment behind the ball.

But funny things begin to happen when you put a long iron into the hands of a high-handicap golfer. If you look in the dictionary for the word "panic," you will see a picture of a high-handicap golfer. What do you do when you are nervous? You tend to speed things up. The natural inclination when hitting a long iron is to swing as quickly as possible in order to simply get it all over with. When you swing quickly, the tendency is for the arms and upper body to outpace the legs, hips, and lower body. In the perfect golf swing, the upper body and lower body are shifting into the downswing in a smooth transition.

If the hips are still turned to the right (for a right-handed golfer) and the arms and upper body have already arrived at the ball, that ball is going to go screaming to the left, usually about ten feet above the ground. By having the clubface slightly open at address, you increase your odds of having a neutral clubface even if your upper body arrives at the ball too soon.

Now, I know what you're thinking. "But what if I swing the long iron in perfect rhythm?" Obviously, the open clubface at address would cause your ball to go to the right of the target. But when was the last time that you hit a long iron with a perfect rhythm? You've got to play the odds. The odds are that your rhythm is not going to be perfect, and your hands are going to arrive before your hips and legs. Take advantage of that slightly open clubface to help keep the shot straight. I can tell you this from years of experience, a nice airborne shot that reaches the green and is twenty feet to the right of the pin is much better than a ball that screams down the left side of the fairway, going lefter and lefterer as it waves goodbye.

There is another reason that pure panic and doubt causes the high-handicap golfer to hit their long iron shots to the left. That is the tightness of their grip. You know from the chapter on the grip and from every instructional book and video that your grip should be light on the club. You've read all the analogies. You should grip the club like you're holding a bird, tight enough that they can't escape, but loose enough so that you don't throttle the bird. Or squeeze the club like you're squeezing an open tube of toothpaste. Tight enough so that you don't drop the tube, but not tight enough that you squeeze out any of the toothpaste.

But try telling your brain that you shouldn't squeeze the club when you are in panic mode. Most high-handicap golfers tend to squeeze the club way too hard. All the golf instructional books and videos point out that the danger of squeezing the club too tightly is that it creates tension in the hands and wrist and doesn't allow the hinging and unhinging of the wrists, which generates power. But the advice from the instructors to have a loose grip actually exacerbates the execution issues for a high-handicap golfer. Because they are told to do it, the high-handicap golfer attempts to have a loose grip when they set up for the shot. But, when the panic of the shot sets in, they squeeze the dickens out of the grip in midswing. That leads to an even greater flaw in the shot.

Let me demonstrate the problem. Pick up a club and take your grip. Make sure that your grip is loose, maybe three to four on a scale of ten. Make sure that the clubface is neutral to the ball.

Now, squeeze the club as hard as you can. Watch what happens to the clubface. Do you see how it immediately closes? So, taking the advice of the pros, the high-handicap golfer's last swing thought is to grip the club loosely. But, somewhere during their backswing or downswing, the panicked brain tells the hands to tighten up and hold on for dear life. What this does is to cause the clubface to close. And that's another reason why you will find it beneficial to have your clubface slightly open as you address the ball. If you find that you don't tense up during the long iron shots and your grip remains loose and the clubhead remains in a neutral position, you're a lucky person. You can get by with having a neutral clubface at address. But if you find your long iron shots turning over and going left (for the right-handed golfer), try setting up with your clubface slightly open at address.

If even that doesn't work, here's one more suggestion I will give you. But this technique is only to be tried if everything else fails. I repeat. Only crack the glass and use this one if nothing else works. When it comes to grip pressure, the optimal solution is to do like the pros do. Have a loose grip when you address the ball and have a loose grip when you make contact with the ball. Failing that, try the technique of opening your clubface at address, so, when your hands inevitably tighten up, they will have the effect of returning the clubface to a neutral position. But if all else fails, go ahead and tighten up your grip before you hit the ball. If your grip is already tight as you address the ball, it can't get any tighter during your swing. If your clubface starts in a neutral position and makes contact with the ball in a neutral position, your ball will go straight.

Now, why do I say that that is a radical solution and only to be used in case of emergency? Because the advice of having a loose grip is a universal tip. Whether you are a good golfer or a bad golfer, you're always going to hit the ball farther if the muscles in your hand and arms are unconstricted. Try this little experiment. Take a baseball in your hand. Grip the baseball as tightly as possible. Now, throw it. Retrieve the ball and hold it in your hand with a loose grip. Allow your wrist to hinge freely. Now, throw the ball again. Unless your body is really unusual, you will always be able to throw the ball significantly farther with a nice, relaxed hand. The same is true for hitting a golf ball.

So, let's accept the fact that using the grip of death on the club is going to prevent your golf shot from going as far as it can versus hitting the ball with a loose grip. But desperate people do desperate things. If you simply cannot swing the club with a loose grip, use the grip of death so that regripping the club at the top doesn't cause your clubface to close, and simply take more club. But hopefully, you will be able to control your fear and hit the ball with a semi-loose grip. Addressing the ball with the slightly open clubface will enable you to hit the ball straight.

One more thought on having the clubface slightly open resulting in you hitting the ball to the right of the target. You may be thinking, "But, my problem isn't whether my clubface is open or closed. I just always seem to hit weak pop-up shots to the first baseman every time I hit a long iron." Let's not get two different problems confused. If you are hitting weak pop-ups to the right, your problem isn't that your clubface isn't aligned neutrally to the ball. Your problem is that you're contacting the ball out on the toe of the club.

Any time you hit a ball off the toe of the club, it's going to create a weak shot to the right. First, you're not hitting the ball in the sweet spot in the center of the club. So, you are losing power to start with. Second, because of the ricochet effect, a ball that hits on the toe of the club (the right side of the clubface as a right-handed golfer faces the flag) will always ricochet out to the right. Third, when you make contact on the toe of the club, it creates a torque effect. When you hit the ball in the center of the clubface, the clubface does not twist to the left or the right. But, when an object comes into contact with something on its right side, it tends to twist to the right. This torque effect opens your clubface and contributes to the weak pop-up shot to the right.

So, don't be afraid to slightly open the clubface on your long iron shots simply because you are currently having a tendency to hit your shots to the right. Go to work on using greater focus and the other techniques in this book, such as the pendulum effect and keeping your elbow close to your side to begin making better contact with the ball on the center of your clubface. Then, you can open the clubface slightly when setting up for your long iron shot without causing the ball to go to the right of the target.

One final thought on opening the clubface slightly on long iron shots. I remember reading an article on Tiger Woods. Tiger said that he opens the clubface slightly for his long iron shots. His reason for doing so is a bit different than ours. Tiger swings his long irons with such amazing speed that he was finding the centrifugal force was closing his clubface. So, when he sets up to the ball, he opens his clubface slightly to compensate. If one of your golf buddies asks why your clubface is open on your long iron shots, just tell them that you are hitting the ball like Tiger Woods!

Another factor which makes it harder for the high-handicap golfer to hit long irons is the longer length of the clubs. For the average set of golf clubs, the long irons are longer than the short irons. Why? It's very simple. Long irons are designed to generate greater distance. The wider the arc of the swing, the greater the distance will be generated. Hey, that's why they call them long irons.

But the farther away from an object we are, the harder it is to make direct contact with that object. That's one of the things that makes golf so difficult. With most sports, the action takes place close to your body. It's easier to hit a tennis ball than a golf ball. First, the length of a tennis racket is shorter than the length of a golf club. That helps. Secondly, the tennis ball is a larger object than a golf ball. And third, the face of the tennis racket is a whole lot bigger and more forgiving than the sweet spot of a golf club. The hockey puck is pretty far away from the hockey player. But the face of the hockey stick is a heck of a lot wider than the sweet spot of the golf club. Bottom line, the farther away from the golfer that the ball is, the more difficult it is to make solid contact with the face of the club.

If the high-handicap golfer finds that the length of the long irons makes it more difficult to hit the ball, you have two options. First, take up handball. Second, choke up on the club. You have probably seen that advice for other clubs. Virtually every instructional book or video is going to suggest that you choke down on your wedges as you get closer to the green. With those wedge shots, distance is not a requirement. Control is king. So, the pros recommend that you choke down on the club for greater control.

Well, the same thing works with your long arms. If you are finding that the greater length of the club is leading to a loss of accuracy, simply choke down a half to a full inch on the club. Granted, that's going to lessen your arc and lead to less distance. Big deal. Take a longer club. Your objective is to maximize the level of control and accuracy in your swing. Therefore, try choking up on your long irons. In fact, when you get to the point where the length of the clubface from your hands is the same with your long iron as it is with your short irons, simply imagine that you are hitting an eight iron instead of a three iron. I'm serious. Most high-handicap golfers swing the short irons relatively well. But, put a three iron in their hand and they can't hit the side of the barn. Some of that is the longer length and the less-forgiving loft of the club. But most of it is mental.

Once the two clubs are the same length, the only difference between the two clubs is the level of the loft. So, don't look at the loft of the club. Simply imagine that you are hitting your favorite eight iron. Swing the club with the same tempo and rhythm and with the same degree of confidence that you swing your shorter irons.

The next issue with long irons is that high-handicap golfers tend to hit the ball thin or fat. Why more so than with the short irons? It's simply the effect that the panic and the lack of confidence has on your ability to focus on the ball.

Let's address a thin shot first. If everything else is constant, the only reason that you will hit a golf ball thin is if the length of your arms changes during the swing. What would cause someone to shorten their arms during the swing? Fear. Pure fear. But, when discussing hitting a ball with a descending blow, I said that the tendency is for high-handicap golfers to extend their arms and hit the ball fat. But my experience is that it is the lowering of the shoulders that causes the arms to extend. Trying to hit down on the ball with a descending blow causes the less-confident golfer to drop their shoulders and lean into the shot. Rarely do high-handicap golfers physically extend their arms in their efforts to rush the shot. I'll address what to do if you are dropping your shoulders when we talk about what causes you to hit the ball fat. But, for now, let us focus on what causes you to hit the ball thin.

Rather than extend the arms during the shot, the panicked golfer actually tends to contract their arms. Don't ask me why. If I was an anthropologist, I would go back to the caveman days. The anthropologist tends to use that to explain all the weird things that we do. Perhaps as part of our "fight or flight" reflexes, when faced with panic, our natural inclination is to pull our arms in to protect our body. Heck, I don't know why we do it. But I have seen too many nervous golfers hit the ball thin when using the confidence-sapping long irons. Watch a first-time golfer. Are they more likely to whiff the ball or chunk the club into the ground behind the ball? They are far more likely to contract their arms and whiff the ball. Go to Topgolf and check it out if you don't believe me.

How do you counteract this effect? When you begin the backswing, purposely extend your arms away from your body. Make sure you have a sensation of extending the arms in a wide arc. And remember, the wider your arc, the farther you will hit the ball.

As for hitting the ball fat, rarely is this due to your arms. Let's face it, it's tough to involuntarily extend your arms out any farther than they are when you address the ball. If you voluntarily attempt to extend your arms, you can do it. But involuntarily extending your arms during the swing? You are more likely to contract your arms.

There are two primary reasons that you hit your long irons fat. First, if you allow your body to sway backward and don't shift your weight back forward, you will hit the ground behind the ball. Virtually every swing will bottom out directly below your body's center of gravity. If you move your center of gravity backward and don't shift it back over the ball (or even better, slightly in front of the ball), your club will bottom out and make contact with the ground behind the ball.

To remedy this, go back and review the chapter on hitting your short irons. The best thing that you can do to avoid swaying back behind the ball is to place your weight on the inside of your trail foot. If your hand-eye coordination is good, you can "fire your hips" and proactively shift your body forward as you begin your downswing. That move is going to give you a lot more power, as it brings into play the powerful muscles in your hips and legs. But not everyone is that coordinated. During your practice sessions, try firing the hips. I provide more detail on how to make this move in the chapter on the driver. If you can pull it off, this will give you more power to your shots and help you make more solid contact at the base of the ball instead of in the ground behind the ball.

As discussed above, the second reason that we hit the long irons fat is we tend to dip our shoulders in the downswing. Remember the pendulum theory. If a pendulum is attached to a constant point, the pendulum will always swing at the same distance from that constant point. If that constant point is lowered, then the pendulum will swing lower. If you drop your shoulders at the top of the backswing or during your downswing, this will cause the base of your pendulum, which is your club head, to swing through lower than it was when you set up to the ball.

What causes us to lower our shoulders? Fear. Pure fear. When our natural instinct is to speed something up in order to get it over quickly, we have a tendency to jerk and lunge forward. By forward, I'm not talking about forward toward the flag. I'm talking about forward in the direction that our body is facing. Our feet are anchored to the ground. There aren't many places that those can go. So, the natural movement is to lean farther into the shot, dropping the shoulders more toward the ball.

There's one other factor that can also cause us to drop our shoulders. As I said earlier in this chapter, we want to hit our long iron shots with a descending blow. Many high-handicappers find it difficult to hit down on the ball with the long iron. So, they have a tendency to overcompensate. Instead of swinging down on the ball with a loose controlled swing, they feel like they have to aggressively swing down on the ball. When they swing down aggressively with their arms, their shoulders have a tendency to follow. This pronounced effort to swing aggressively down on the ball causes us to drop our shoulders as we lunge toward the ball.

What can we do to prevent the dropping of our shoulders? Utilize a swing thought to initiate your backswing of maintaining your setup posture throughout the entire swing. When I find myself dipping my shoulders, I repeat to myself right before hitting the ball, "Stay high in the saddle." It has nothing to do with a John Wayne movie. It simply means that I want to maintain my posture, keep my backbone as straight as possible, and not drop my shoulders during the swing. The important point here is to have that swing thought prior to initiating the swing. Remember, one of the biggest problems that high-handicappers have is that they tend to have too many thoughts swirling around in their brain during the swing. Fortunately, this is a swing thought that you can have prior to initiating the swing. Maybe it's another form of muscle memory. But, if we think about staying high in the saddle, that thought remains with us as we undertake the swing.

Unfortunately, you might have noted that this swing thought is completely the opposite of the swing thought of extending the arms out through the swing. But if you think about it, it seems only natural that the two swing thoughts should run counter to each other, as we are fighting two different and opposite problems. The swing thought of extending the arms is used if we are hitting the ball thin. The swing thought of staying high in the saddle is used if we are hitting the ball fat. Utilize the swing thought that is most required for the problem you are having most often. If you tend to hit the ball fat, think about staying high in the saddle. If you tend to hit the ball thin, think about extending the arms. But if you get into the round of golf and the opposite of your usual problem is occurring, don't be afraid to change your swing thought during the round.

Finally, when it comes to long irons, don't forget the number one technique in this book. Focus. Focus. Focus. Before you hit the ball, go through a mental checklist of the things that you want to do. Think about where the ball should go in your stance. Think about how you want to distribute your weight (generally, evenly divided between both legs for a long iron shot). Think about how you want to brace your weight on the inside of your trail foot. Think about whether you need to initiate the shot by extending your arms away from your body or staying high in the saddle. Take your practice swing behind the ball. Address the ball and take your practice swing waggle. Then forget all your swing thoughts! Focus on a spot on the back of the ball. Take your backswing and focus on swinging down and through the ball.

This exaggerated focus is extremely important in your long iron shots. Why? Panic. Panic is the enemy of focus. You are more likely to panic when swinging the club where technique is much more important, your margin of error is decreased, and you lack confidence in your ability to pull off the shot. Therefore, you must overcome the effects of the panic. And the best way to do that is through an incredible focus on making solid contact with the ball.

THE HYBRIDS

The invention of the hybrid clubs has been one of the greatest benefits for the high-handicap golfer. Many golfers who struggle to hit their long irons or their fairway metals are able to dramatically improve their golf swing by using a hybrid. Ironically, I am probably going to spend the least amount of time discussing the hybrids.

The reason for this is that the purpose of the hybrid is to enable a golfer to use a club type they are more comfortable with. Therefore, the tips that can help with hitting the hybrid are contained within the chapter on using the club you are more comfortable with.

Let me explain. Let's say that a golfer struggles with the long irons. Ironically, golfers who have difficulty hitting irons tend to be more comfortable with fairway metals. Conversely, golfers who struggle to hit fairway metals tend to be more comfortable with irons. Why is that? I've read many articles and books that attempt to explain this phenomenon. Frankly, golfers struggle with the explanation, simply because it's a mental thing. However, here's the best explanation I can offer. Iron shots tend to be based on hitting with a descending blow.

Fairway metals tend to be based on hitting a more sweeping shot. Mentally, golfers simply seem to be more comfortable with one technique or the other. If they are very good at hitting a descending blow with the club, it is difficult for them to transfer their shot to one in which they are required to simply sweep across the ground. And vice versa.

Enter the hybrid. Hybrid simply means that something is halfway between one thing and another. So, a hybrid is simply a club that is halfway between a long iron and a fairway metal. If a golfer struggles with hitting a descending blow with their long iron but is more comfortable with the sweeping technique of the fairway metal, they simply use a hybrid and swing the club like a fairway metal. Conversely, if the golfer struggles with the sweeping motion of the fairway metals, they simply hit the hybrid like a glorified long iron.

Therefore, the first thing you want to do is determine the technique you are more comfortable with. After years of experimentation, I discovered that I am more comfortable with the sweeping motion of a fairway metal than I am with the descending blow of a long iron. So, when I added the first hybrid to my bag, my stroke more resembled my swing of the fairway metal than it did the long iron. So, the best techniques for compensating for your lack of hand-eye coordination can be found in the respective chapter on hitting long irons or fairway metals.

My parting advice on hybrids, though, is if you are not using them, you should. But before you buy one, take advantage of the free swing analysis offered to you by most golf shops. First, swing the hybrid like you would a long iron. Make a mental note of the statistics provided by the analytical equipment. Next, swing the club with the sweeping motion of the fairway metals. Again, note your statistics. Feel free to ask the golf professional their opinion of your performance with the hybrid. That is what they are paid to do. But remember, their objective is to sell you that club! So, really probe deeply. Ask lots of questions. Make them earn their money! Using the feedback from the swing analysis, utilize the techniques outlined in this book under long irons and fairway metals to maximize your performance with the hybrids.

THE FAIRWAY METALS

Fairway metals are the most puzzling clubs in the bag. If you do a survey of high-handicap golfers, almost all of them struggle with sand shots. Most struggle with their wedges around the green. And long irons are generally feared by high-handicap golfers.

But when it comes to fairway metals, we find some high-handicap golfers who struggle with the fairway metals, while other golfers swear by them. In my chapter on hybrids, I gave you my theory that high-handicap golfers tend to fall in one of two camps. Either they are more comfortable with the descending blow of a long iron shot, or they prefer the sweeping shot associated with the fairway metal. This dichotomy of half the golfers liking the swing of the fairway metals and the other half struggling with the clubs reinforces my theory.

Regardless of whether you are good or bad at hitting your fairway metals, allow me to provide a few suggestions that might help. First, let's talk about the sweeping motion. There may be some of you reading this book who didn't realize that that's what you were supposed to be doing. After all, the fairway metal swing is radically different from the iron swing. I recall one of the very first instructional articles I read in one of the golf magazines showed an illustration of a golfer holding a broom. The article pointed out how the fairway wood (at that time) shot should be a low and slow swing similar to the motion of sweeping the floor.

Should you take a divot with your fairway metal? Actually, the jury is out on that one. While most instructors would tell you to sweep the ball off the surface without taking a divot, there are dissenters. Lee Trevino famously hit his fairway woods (at the time) with more of a descending blow, taking a nice toupee. The method that you should use is going to depend a lot on how well you swing your fairway metals.

If you are not making good solid contact with the ball on your fairway metal shots, generally one of two things is happening. First, you are hitting the ball fat. Your clubface is striking the turf behind the ball rather than making clean contact with the ball. Alternatively, you are hitting the ball thin. The front edge of the fairway metal is making contact with the belly of the ball.

If you are having trouble with either of these errors, you need to look at the mechanics of your swing. If you are hitting the ball fat, this generally means that your swing is too steep. In other words, you are lifting the club up in more of a V-shaped swing rather than a sweeping U-shaped swing. The descending club head is making contact with the ground at the bottom portion of your V-shaped swing. If your swing is off, it has one of two effects. First, if the point of contact is slightly behind the ball (or dramatically behind the ball for many of us!), you have the famous fat shot.

But it can go the other way. If the point of descent of your V-shaped swing is in front (as defined by the point of the ball closest to the pin), you get the famous "karate chop" shot. Now be honest. I know you've done it before. You make contact with the ball. The ball appears to make contact with the ground about an inch in front of where it originally sat and bounces embarrassingly about twenty feet in front of you. You scratch your head and say, "That was weird. I wonder why it did that." Well, it's quite simple. Your clubface came down sharply upon the top of the ball. It doesn't make contact with the equator of the ball. So, it isn't the normal thin shot which sends the ball out about one hundred yards, but never more than ten feet from the ground. Because the karate chop shot is coming down on the ball, it simply drives it into the turf in front of the ball, taking all of the forward momentum out of the shot, and resulting in the twenty-foot blooper.

If you hit either the fat shot or the karate chop, you need to develop more of a sweeping swing. In your backswing, bring the club head back "low and slow." Consciously feel your arms remaining extended out away from your body. Imagine that you are knocking over objects at least six inches behind the ball. In fact, in your drill, line up a few tees behind the ball. See how many you can take out. After the low and slow takeaway, keep the extension in your arms as the club winds around your body.

At the top, make sure your front arm (the left arm for a right-handed golfer) is as straight as possible. Your trailing arm has to bend. In order to keep your trailing arm elbow close to your body, your arm has to hinge at the elbow. So, focus on keeping your front arm as straight as possible. Swing to the top and freeze. You want to have the sensation that your hands are as far away from your head as they can be. Most high-handicap golfers aren't the most flexible people in the world. There will be some bend at the elbow. But try to keep your front arm as straight as possible.

Try not to let your arm bend at the elbow. That is a shot killer for two reasons. First, your poor contact with the ball is due to the V-shaped swing. Allowing your arms to collapse contributes to the V-shaped swing. The straighter your arm is at the top, the wider your swing arc will be. Keeping your arm straight will create a wide swing arm and the U-shaped swing needed to make solid contact with the ball.

Second, remember that speed is generated by a wide arc and the hinging effect of your wrists. If your front arm bends

With fairway metals, keep the front arm as straight as possible. This will generate the widest arc and the most speed. Note also how I am bracing against the back foot. This prevents swaying.

significantly at the elbow, you reduce the width of your swing arc. But, the very important hinging of your wrist is reduced as your whole arm is collapsing at the top. So, when you freeze your backswing at the top, check to make sure that your front arm is as straight as possible, your hands are as far away from your head as they can be, and your wrists are freely hinging at the top. This will result in the U-shaped swing that you need to make good contact with the ball.

Once you reach the apex of your backswing, initiate the downswing, but with the same sensation simply in reverse. Imagine the clubface descending approximately six inches behind the ball and sweeping through the ball without making contact with the dirt. Make contact with the grass as the club sweeps under the ball. But don't make serious contact with the dirt. That's the essence of the sweeping swing.

Let's assume that your problem is not that you are hitting the ball fat or doing the karate chop. Instead, your problem is the good old-fashioned thin shot. Try as you might, you simply are not able to sweep the club underneath the ball. I went through a spell where this happened. At one point, I was pretty good with the fairway metals. I bought a new set of three and five fairway metals. My problem was that I started to think about how I was swinging down. Instead of just intuitively swinging through the ball, I was thinking about where I made contact. All of a sudden, I could not get the clubface down under the ball to save my life. The harder I tried, the worse it got.

My theory as to why that happens is that good old panic sets in. I suddenly lost confidence in my swing. Whereas originally, I stood over the fairway metal shot with a high degree of confidence that I would be able to pull it off, all of a sudden, fear gripped me every time I stood over the shot. For whatever reason, fear tends to cause us to contract our arms. Try as hard as I could to keep my arms extended through the shot, my arms would contract, shortening the length of my pendulum and resulting in one thin shot after another.

If you want to continue to use a sweeping swing for your fairway woods, below I will provide several tips that can help you out. But at the end of the day, if you've tried all of these techniques and you continue to hit the ball thin, let me give you the "Break the glass, use only in the event of an emergency" tip. Hit it like Lee Trevino. Use a more descending blow for your fairway metal shots. Take a nice divot in front of the ball. Granted, you could potentially develop one of the two flaws that I pointed out earlier that can result from a V-shaped swing. The descending blow could cause you to hit the ball fat, or it could result in the karate chop.

At this point, you simply have to "pick your poison." If you simply cannot break the habit of hitting the ball thin with a sweeping swing, my advice would be to try the more descending V-shaped swing. If you are karate chopping the ball, this means that your swing has too much of a V-shape. Shallow out your swing. Don't go all the way back to the U-shaped swing. But find another letter of the alphabet that falls somewhere between the U and V. (Just joking. There isn't one.) Avoid the karate chop swing at all costs.

If you find that using the V-shaped swing is causing you to hit the ball fat, simply move the location of the ball in your stance back a full inch. That may sound like a Mickey Mouse solution. But, hey, you are already in emergency mode. Move the ball back in your stance, take the best semi-descending swing that you can, and let the clubface make contact on the back of the ball. It's a much better outcome than hitting the ball thin, fat, or with the karate chop.

There are a few other techniques that can help you with the execution of the fairway metal shot. First, you'll remember the dreaded sway. Because the fairway metal is a much longer club and it is utilizing a more sweeping swing, it takes longer to execute than a short iron or wedge shot. Unfortunately, this additional time at your disposal tends to lead to negative things like swaying your body backward in the shot. You have to fight this tendency to sway back in your shot. Remember, swaying backward moves your center of balance backward in your shot. If you're still on your back foot when you make contact with the ball or haven't moved your body back in a forward momentum, you're going to hit behind the ball.

Therefore, the tip about feeling your weight on the inside of your back foot becomes even more critically important in the fairway metal shot. In your final practice swing, make sure that you feel your weight on the inside of your back foot.

Next, remember the tip about keeping the elbow of your trailing arm as close to your midsection as possible. Just like with the sway, the longer length of the fairway metal and the sweeping motion encourages the golfer to allow the elbow to disengage from their body into the famous "chicken wing" swing. While it is virtually impossible to keep your elbow actually touching your midsection during the sweeping swing of the fairway metal, mentally and physically, the more you can keep your trail arm close to the body as it hinges, the better your pendulum effect will work.

How far back you swing the club when hitting a fairway metal is a matter of opinion. It's sort of like how far back you take the club when driving the ball. John Daly swings it back so far that the club head practically touches the ground. Most instructors say to go back to parallel and no farther. Many high-handicap golfers find that taking the driver back less than parallel gives them greater control. All of this is true for the fairway wood. You will see some pros take the fairway wood beyond parallel. Many of them stop at parallel. But I'm going to encourage you to take the fairway wood back less than parallel. Why? Because the fairway metal shot is most likely from the turf, and not from on a tee. Therefore, you have less margin for error with the fairway wood. The greater control offered by a shorter backswing will benefit you significantly.

Do you want to use the same L-shaped technique that I have advocated for the short and long irons? Experiment. Frankly, I think that the same technique of feeling that your arms are coming up to about 9:00 on the clock face with the fairway metal club hinged back at a 90° angle will lead to better contact with this club. Are you feeling like that will rob you of needed power? Because, after all, fairway metals are power clubs. Well, remember that, even though you are having the sensation that you are only bringing your arms back halfway in the swing, in reality, your arms will go back farther. Videotaping your swing will confirm this.

My best advice is to simply experiment. Try bringing your club back different lengths and see which length results in the most accurate and powerful shot. But always favor accuracy over power! Yes, the fairway metal is considered a power club. You want to advance the ball down the fairway as far as possible. But in power versus accuracy for a pro, we are talking about the ball ending up in different locations on the fairway. If your fairway metal shot is not accurate, we're not talking about the shot being in one of multiple locations on the fairway. We are talking about your shot being in the woods, in the lake, or in the hazards. Use experimentation to develop a technique that provides power, but with the mandatory accuracy.

There's one other tip that I can give you that doesn't really apply that much to any other club other than, perhaps, the long irons. That tip is to swing through the ball. One of the biggest mistakes that many high-handicap golfers make is that, even after taking a nice low slow backswing and swinging in a nice sweeping motion, they tend to yank the club back up in the follow-through. This can tend to lead to another variation of the karate chop. Despite the low slow backswing, your clubface is starting to ascend too early in the swing. Hitting the back of the ball in this ascending method creates a ricochet effect that simply drives the ball into the turf in front of its original position.

Therefore, have a mental picture of making contact with the ball and continuing the low motion of your backswing and downswing out through the ball. A good technique is to envision knocking down several objects, such as golf tees, placed in front of the ball. After sweeping the ball through the club and along the ground in front of the ball, allow the clubface to continue swinging up and around your body in a beautiful arc. Many golfers find that holding their "pose" at the top of the swing enables them to properly extend through the ball and down the line. Simply imagine that you are posing for the cover of *Golf* magazine!

Here are two final tips. I have given these tips for other clubs. However, errors seem to be magnified with the fairway metals because of their longer lengths and the longer time required for the sweeping swing. The first of these is focus. Once you have worked through all of your swing thoughts and established your muscle memory and your practice swing, BEFORE you take your real swing, clear your mind of all swing thoughts. The only thing that you want to focus on is the back of the ball. Keep that focus on the back of the ball all the way through your swing.

Finally, slow down. Because it is a power club, or because most high-handicap golfers are nervous about hitting their fairway metals, they tend to swing them way too quickly. Slow down. The distance you gain from hitting the ball in the sweet spot at the middle of your clubface is going to make much more of an effect on the length of your shot than the speed with which your clubface is moving. So, slow down and make solid contract with the ball. In hitting a fairway metal, I find that the most effective final swing thought before beginning the swing is always, "low and slow." Give it a try.

GETTING OUT OF
THE SANDBOX

If you ask high-handicap golfers what the most terrifying shot in golf is, the answer will be almost universal. It is the shot from the greenside bunker. And yet the pros will tell you that if there is any kind of rough around the green, they would much rather be in the sandbox. How can there be such a wide diversity of opinion on the relative difficulty of the sand shot?

The answer is that the professional and good amateur golfer have two things that you don't when it comes to the sand shot. First, they have good technique. A bunker shot is one of the most technique-oriented shots. Generally, you change your stance, your weight distribution, the angle of the clubface, the track of the club through the ball, and the speed with which you swing the club. The good golfers know the proper technique with which to get the ball safely out of the sand. In fact, their goal with the bunker shot is totally different than yours. Your goal is just to get out of the sand and onto the green. Their goal is to get the ball as close as possible to the flag. They even have a statistic for this, called sand saves. If you look at the stats for the winner of the professional tournaments, the winning golfer generally gets the ball out of the sand, and one putts almost every sand shot.

Second, the good golfer has confidence that they will successfully get the ball out of the sand and close to the flag. We all know how important it is to have confidence to be a good golfer. Even a golfer with the best technique in the world, if they don't have confidence that they're going to be able to pull off the shot, will manage to mangle their technique. Otherwise, why do you find so many golfers who have a two handicap on the driving range, but an eighteen handicap on the course? When the driving range shot carries no risk of failure, their proper technique comes through. But under the stress and tension of the shot out on the course, especially when there's money involved, all the little seeds of doubt creep into their head. That confidence flies out the door. Since so many things can go wrong with a bunker shot, it is probably the shot where the lack of confidence has the most severe consequences for the bad golfer.

Therefore, our object is to provide you with the proper technique. Then, your job is to hit the practice range and practice, practice, and practice that technique until it comes as second nature. Then, and only then, will you walk into the bunker with a high degree of confidence that you're going to get your ball out.

Now, notice something very important about the statement that I just made. I mentioned earlier that the objective of the good golfer is to get their ball out of the bunker and as close to the flag as possible. Our objective is going to be much simpler. As we begin to master the sand shot, our goal is simply to get the ball out of the bunker and onto the green. For now, getting out of the bunker and taking a two-putt is fine. Long term, as you continue to practice the shot with the correct technique, you can work on getting the ball closer and closer to the pin. But let's not bite off too much or you're going to be frustrated with the process. Set your goal low, master that technique, and then you can begin to raise the bar.

Consistent with the theme of this book, I'm not going to spend a lot of time discussing the basics of the sand shot. With one major exception, your technique is going to be identical to the good golfer. Any good golf instructional book, video series, or lesson from the pro is going to take you through the best technique. Whole books have been written just on bunker shots. (I know, I have several!)

So, let's quickly go over a couple of basics and then get to the heart of the matter, the secret shot. Although some pros offer different variations of the basic sand shot, most will include the following. An open stance is generally recommended. The bunker shot is one of the few shots where you do want to have an outside-in swing as you come across the ball. This means that as you begin your backswing, the clubface is going to be more up in the air in front of you and not so much wrapped around your body. This is one of the few shots where you are going to need to disengage the elbow of your back arm from your midsection. Having the open stance gives you an easier route to raise the clubface up more in the air and enter the clubface into the sand with an out-to-in stroke.

Next, you will always need to dig your feet down into the sand. There's no magic to this move. I'm sure you have seen the pros do it hundreds of times. After taking your stance, you simply waggle your feet back and forth until they dig into the sand approximately a quarter to half an inch. There is one little thing about digging your feet in that I would like to point out.

Digging your shoes into the sand gives you a unique opportunity to gauge the dynamics of the sand. As you know, you're not allowed to touch the sand with your club or any other part of your body, except your feet. So, your feet become a valuable source of information.

As you waggle your feet back and forth to dig into the sand, pay attention to the type of sand you're working with. First, is the sand dry, light, and fluffy or is it wet and thickly packed? That's going to impact your shot. Your clubface tends to move more smoothly through light fluffy sand. But, if the sand is wet and compact, it begins to resemble more of your concrete driveway. The clubface has more of a tendency to not dig into the sand, but rather to slide through the sand, taking a very thin strip of sand. If you don't prepare for this, it can lead to disaster as you watch your ball sailing over the green. If the sand feels denser, you will need to take more of a descending blow in order to penetrate the sand and dig beneath the ball.

If you find it very difficult to dig your shoes down to between a quarter and half an inch, that could mean that there just isn't a whole lot of sand in the bunker. That's what you get for playing the cheap muni! Again, you may need to compensate for that layer of concrete lurking beneath the thin layer of sand by taking more of a descending blow with the club.

Opinions vary on weight distribution. However, most pros suggest that you place more of your weight on your front foot. If the weight is evenly distributed, players have a bad habit of swaying back and hitting too far behind the ball. Good golfers like to take an aggressive shot from the sand. Leaning forward and coming down sharply with the club gives them the aggressive shot that they are looking for. But just because that works for them doesn't mean that it will work for you.

So, like everything else in this book, experiment. Try shots leaning forward with your weight on your front foot. Then, try some shots with an even distribution of your weight. See what works best for you.

The universal rule of hitting a sand shot is to open the clubface. Opening a clubface is always a technique to get greater height on the ball. Why? Because you are adding more loft to the club. The basic sand wedge is going to be approximately a 56° angle. Watch what happens to the clubface when you open it up. That angle moves more and more toward a 90° angle, which you would have if the clubface was totally flat to the ground beneath.

Why is an open clubface beneficial in the sand shot? First, it's important to understand the dynamics of the design of the sand wedge. We have Walter Hagen to thank for the revolutionary design of the sand wedge. In the old days, the pros simply used another lofted club. But in an effort to hit behind the ball, regular clubs had a tendency to dig into the sand. Taking too much sand resulted in the ball not going far enough. Many an early sand shot was frustratingly left in the sand. As the story goes, Walter Hagen noticed how airplane wings were designed in a way that forced air under the wing in order to provide lift for the plane. He designed the first sand wedge by adding a flange at the bottom of the club. If you look at your sand wedge, compared to any other club in your bag, it's dramatically different. This flange at the bottom of the club causes the club to slide through the sand rather than down into the sand. Just like the airplane wing slicing through the air, this design element enables the sand wedge to slide through the sand at the proper depth, lifting a layer of sand and, hopefully your ball, out on a magic carpet of flying sand.

But even with the revolutionary design of the sand wedge and its ability to slide through the sand, the sand wedge still needs a little help. If the edge of the sand wedge is neutral, it has a tendency to smack down into the sand. There's simply too much mass of metal making contact with the sand all at once. So, what you want to have happen is for the metal to make contact with the sand in a very small area. Then, like the camel's nose in the tent, the rest of the clubface eventually arrives at that point in the sand. If you hold up the clubface and move your grip around to create an open face, you see that you have minimized the amount of the clubface making initial contact with the sand. That's the first benefit of an open clubface.

The next benefit of an open clubface is the loft that we discussed earlier. There are numerous reasons why you want your ball to rise dramatically after the shot. First, sand bunkers tend to have rims around them. In some cases, when golf courses are designed by very sadistic people, the golfer might find themselves hitting into a wall of additional sand. Think of the road hole at St Andrews. In order to avoid this wall of sand or the grassy ridge that surrounds the bunker, you want to lift the ball high into the air.

Next, unless you're a really good golfer, it's hard to control the amount of roll that your ball is going to have after it lands on the green. The amount of role is determined by the speed of the ball, which is determined by the amount of sand that you hit before the ball was lifted out of the bunker. Because you're struggling just to make contact with the sand behind the ball, forget about being able to have a significant level of control of how much sand you take. If the ball comes out low, it has a tendency to roll farther. That makes your final location very unpredictable. Balls that are hit higher into the air with an open-faced club tend to roll less after landing. That's what you want. You want to have the ball high in the air, landing like a butterfly just short of the hole, and rolling gradually up to the pin. Thus, the open face for the club is recommended.

One major mistake that many high-handicap golfers make when they attempt to open the club is they try to manipulate the clubface open using their hands. In other words, they will start with a neutral clubface and then simply turn their hands to the right (assuming a right-handed golfer) to open the clubface. What's wrong with this? Remember, one of the main principles of the physics of a golf shot is that the hands will always return to a neutral position. So, if you are manually opening the clubface as you swing back down from the back-swing, your hands will revert to a neutral position, closing the face of the club back to a neutral position. So, when you are setting up for the sand shot, turn the club to have an open face and then take a neutral grip on the club.

Now that we have reinforced the basics of the sand shot, which you are going to execute just like the good golfers, let's get to the secret technique for high-handicap golfers. Before we learn the secret technique, let's delve further into why the technique given to you by the good golfer with great hand-eye coordination doesn't work for you. The basic technique for hitting a bunker shot, as taught to you by good golfers, is to bring the club head down and hit the sand approximately two to three inches behind the ball. That's relatively easy to do for people with good hand-eye coordination. But if you are reading this book, I know you can't do that. You know you can't do that. Your playing partners know you can't do that. So, what do you do? Stop trying!

Yes, you heard me correctly. Simply stop trying to hit the sand two to three inches behind the ball. Instead, we are going to use an alternative and incredibly simple technique. In the introduction, I said that good golfers will laugh at some of the techniques in this book. This technique will cause them to have spasms of laughter, resulting in them falling to the floor. But who cares? The reason that they are laughing is because they can't understand why high-handicap golfers can't simply do what they do, aim the clubface two to three inches behind the ball. But you've tried it thousands of times. For people with less than stellar hand-eye coordination, it simply doesn't work.

Despite the fact that pros would laugh at our secret technique, this technique actually came from a professional golfer. In fact, it came from one of the best professional golfers ever. This technique, which frankly I think is the best technique I've ever read in a golf magazine, came from none other than Tom Watson. I am pretty sure that Tom Watson has incredible hand-eye coordination. So, if Tom Watson has no trouble hitting the sand two to three inches behind the ball, then why would he be the source of one of the most effective techniques for those who can't pull this off? I think it's the nature of instruction and golf magazines. When the editors asked Tom for an effective technique, he realized that the magazine was read by many people who were not blessed with his level of talent. So, he developed a technique that can easily be used by our less-talented selves.

Here's how it works. Remember the pendulum effect? That is the very basic principle of physics that causes an item that is anchored at one end to swing to the same spot every time. In a regular golf shot, where our feet are level with the ball, we hope that our swaying returns to where it starts, at the base of the ball. But what Tom Watson noticed was that if we dig our feet into the ground by half an inch and the golf club returns to the same spot level with their feet, then the golf club will now swing back to a half-inch below the ball! Voila!

If you think about it, the principles of this solution are very simple. The traditional method requires a high-handicap golfer who can barely make pure contact with the back of the ball on a regular swing to aim and hit the sand at a precise point behind the ball. If you are still reading this book, your ability to do this is limited. But, if you are able to take a regular swing and the position of your feet below the ball causes you to hit two to three inches behind the ball, then anybody can pull off this shot.

While the physics of the situation dictate that the clubface that is returning to where it started will slide approximately one-half inch below the sand, there's one other thing that you want to do to ensure the success of the shot. That is to listen for the "thud." I wish I could explain to you the physics of the importance of the thud. But unfortunately, I can't. This is one technique where I can't explain to you why it works or why it is important. You just have to take my word that it works. If you bring the club down to the proper place behind the ball with the face wide open and the flange of the club ready to slide underneath the ball, you will hear a sound that can best be described as a thud.

While I can't explain the importance of the thud from a scientific perspective, I can tell you its importance from the mental aspect of confidence. When you hear the thud, it is a mental reassurance that the shot has been done correctly. The distinctive sound tells you that the flat part of the bottom of the flange has made solid contact with the sand. Then, the physics kick in and the clubface slides beneath the ball. When you go out to practice the shot, before you even lay down the first ball in the sand, practice the shot. Listen for the thud. Ingrain that sound in your brain. Then drop a ball, utilize the other techniques that we've discussed, and listen for that distinctive thud as you execute one beautiful sand shot after another.

We now know exactly the swing that we want to achieve. So, forget about trying to aim the clubface to make contact three inches behind the ball. Simply set up with the ball in the middle of your stance. Then, dig your shoes half an inch into the sand. Take a regular golf swing (with a little bit of an out-to-in swing path as we discussed earlier). What happens is that as it descends, the clubface naturally strikes the sand approximately two to three inches behind the ball. Listen for the thud. The clubface then slides under the ball at the optimal depth of about a quarter to a half an inch. Importantly, no part of the clubface makes any contact with the ball (a common occurrence when we are trying to aim the clubface to contact the sand a certain distance behind the ball). After sliding under the ball, the clubface naturally emerges on the other side of the ball. The first thing that we notice is that we have created that dollar bill-size divot in the sand that the pros encourage us to make. Secondly, we watch the ball fly out of the sand on that magic carpet of granules.

I know this technique sounds kind of crazy. We are completely throwing out the basic technique that the pros teach and use. But this compensatory technique really, really works. Try to contain your excitement. Pick up your sand wedge and head to your nearest practice bunker. After you set up in the bunker and work your shoes into the ground, simply take a normal swing, as if the ball was in the middle of the fairway. Let the physics do their job. You will be amazed that you make solid contact with the sand and send the ball on a high arc onto the green. Most importantly, after hitting this shot over and over again and seeing that it works every time, your confidence in your sand shot ability will grow. I can't say that you'll get to the point where, like the pros, you would rather be in the sand than in the fringe. But, don't be surprised if you get to that point.

Now that we have mastered the basic greenside bunker shot, we need to look at two variations. First, we'll look at the green side bunker shot where the flag is quite a long way away. Or the even more treacherous shot where you have another bunker or wide area of grass before you get to the green and the flag. Second, we'll look at the fairway bunker shot.

Let's begin with the long greenside bunker shot. Basically, your technique for the shot is going to be identical to your technique for the shorter greenside bunker shots, with a few minor deviations. First, if the hole isn't too far away, we're going to stick with the sand wedge. But instead of opening up the clubface, you want to keep it neutral. Remember all that stuff I told you about wanting to get the ball lofted as high as possible coming out of the sand? Well, forget all that. You don't have that luxury with the long shot. If you lift the ball high into the air and it settles on the green with very little roll, you're never going to get your ball to the hole that's farther away. Now, you need that low flying shot.

Some golfers stick with the sand wedge regardless of how far away the flag is. They simply take a longer backswing and/ or attempt to swing faster. However, a longer backswing and a faster swing is a quick recipe for disaster for the less-talented golfer. So, we're going to use another method to compensate. Substitute a pitching wedge or even a nine iron for your sand wedge. Why does that help? It's a matter of loft. Remember that the lower the number of the iron that you use, the less loft that it has. Less loft in a club translates into longer distance. So, if you find that, even after you close your clubface on your sand wedge to a more neutral position, you're still having trouble getting the ball to the hole, try a less lofted club.

There's one more technique for the longer greenside bunker shot. When you have a shorter shot, you will tend to have a V-shaped swing. On a short sand shot, you don't want to make too clean of a contact with the ball. If you do, it will shoot across the green. You want to take lots of sand to cushion the blow. If you swing with a shallow arc, you don't get enough sand. You want the club head to penetrate into the sand. This is especially important if the sand is wet or thick. You don't want the club head to skim across the sand. So, you take a V-shaped swing and hit down on the sand with a descending blow. But with a longer shot, you are going to need to generate a bit more power. And you don't want to catch too much sand, thus eroding the power of your swing. In order to achieve that, your backswing will be more of a U-shape. You will consciously think of the clubface taking a shallower path, skimming under the ball and launching the ball out on a longer flight.

But be very careful with this shot. Practice your longer greenside bunker shot. If the use of this U-shaped, shallow, and faster stroke causes your shot to be more erratic, then ditch it! Pros and good amateurs use a more upright backswing because their goal is to get the ball as close as possible to the pin. They need this technique and the added speed that it generates to get the ball all the way to the pin. Also, their faster swing speed results in them putting a lot of spin on the ball. Basically, they are using the grit of the sand like sandpaper to create a lot of friction, resulting in back spin. So, their shot tends to fly closer to the pin where the backspin causes it to stop quickly, hopefully nestled up against the pin. But you do not generate that much speed. Remember, speed causes inaccuracy. You are better off having a slower swing, but more accurate contact. Without the backspin created by the pros, your best strategy is to get the ball about halfway to the flag and then let it roll the rest of the way.

Try speeding up your swing and carrying the ball closer to the flag. But if the use of this technique is creating a more unreliable swing (and eroding your confidence), then it is not worth it. Simply stick with the secret technique, but utilize the neutral face of the club and, perhaps, a little bit longer and a little bit faster U-shaped swing to get the ball as close to the flag as possible. I'll bet if you're able to get out of the sand and be able to putt after taking that long greenside bunker shot, it's a significant improvement over what you're doing now!

We're not going to spend a lot of time on the fairway bunker. Again, the technique that you use is going to be similar to the one used by the pros. Any instructor is going to tell you the basics. You are still going to want to dig your shoes into the sand. Importantly, though, you are digging your shoes into the sand in the fairway bunker for a different reason than why you dig in for the greenside bunker. Rather than digging in to cause the clubface to slide under the ball, digging into the sand for a fairway bunker is really more designed to give you more stability in the shot. Get your shoes past the surface sand, which causes you to slip and slide down to the base of firm dirt underneath the sand.

Next, set up with the ball farther back in your stance. Why? Because in a fairway bunker shot, you don't want to carry the ball out on a magic carpet of sand. When your clubface collides with the sand, it slows down the clubface speed. That's why you can swing pretty quickly in a greenside bunker and the ball only comes out and rolls about ten or twenty feet. But, if you utilize that technique in a fairway bunker where you may be one hundred or more yards from the flag, you'll never get there. So, in a fairway bunker, you are actually going to make contact with the ball before you make contact with the sand. Moving the ball back in your stance helps to guarantee that you make contact with the ball first, rather than the sand.

Here's another change that you need to make. When you take your grip on the club, you will need to cheat down the handle at least half an inch to an inch. Why? Well, remember the basic physics of the secret technique? If you dig down into the sand, your clubface is going to go into the sand behind the ball. You don't want that to happen on a fairway bunker shot. You want the clubface to make contact with the ball. So, cheating down half an inch on the grip of the club compensates for the half inch of lower altitude that you have gained when you dig your shoes into the ground.

Finally, there is one more change in your technique that you will need to make. In a regular golf shot, you're going to have a lot of natural movement from your lower body. In a greenside bunker shot, you're going to find that you have a lot of lower body movement also. The lower body movement is fine as long as it enables the club head to slide gracefully under the ball. But, in a fairway bunker shot, you have much less margin for error. If your body sways back, you'll have a tendency to strike the sand behind the ball. As we've already discussed, this is going to make it awfully hard for your ball to travel the distance it needs to get on the green.

If your lower body sways forward, you're going to make contact with the belly of the ball. Now, we have all played with that incredibly lucky golfer who contacts the belly of the ball, and you watch in horror as it skirts across the ground and comes to rest on the green. But that's not a good technique to utilize on a consistent basis. You need to go with the odds. Your goal is to make solid contact at the base of your ball prior to the clubface entering the sand. The best technique to achieve this is to try to take the lower body out of the shot as much as possible. Once you have taken your stance, lock up your knees and legs. Take the swing utilizing only the upper body. It's a tough technique to master, but with some practice, you'll get better at it.

Finally, with all of these other alterations to the basic shot, you're going to need to take one more compensatory step. The net effect of these techniques, primarily taking your lower body out of the shot, is going to result in your ball flying less distance than it normally would with that particular club. So, you are definitely going to need to take at least one and, possibly, two extra clubs. If you normally hit your nine iron one hundred and ten yards (Pros, please do not laugh at that. That really is how far we hit our nine irons!) and your fairway bunker shot is one hundred and ten yards from the hole, you may need to drop to an eight iron or even a seven iron.

Finding a fairway bunker on your practice facility may be difficult. It's a little tough to practice this shot on your standard driving range. Their bunkers tend to be located beside the practice green. Not the best place to be hitting one hundred-yard shots. But, if you can find a driving range or a practice area at your golf club that has a bunker where you can hit all out, take advantage of it. Hit a few shots from outside of the bunker. Then climb into the bunker with that same club and see where your ball goes. Most likely, it will fall ten to twenty yards shorter. Now, go up one club and hit from the sand again. Keep trying longer clubs until the distance of your sand shot is similar to the distance from the grass shot.

If you just can't find a place to practice fairway bunker shots, this experimentation may have to take place on the actual course. But if the first time you are out on the course after reading this book and you find you are in a bunker one hundred and ten yards from the hole, replace the nine iron with an eight iron. Utilize the techniques that we've discussed. If the worst thing that happens to you is that your shot ends up ten yards short of the hole, you're probably going to be thrilled. And remember to pull out the seven iron the next time you end up in that bunker!

THE DRIVER

If you are reading this book to learn how to hit your drives three hundred yards, you're reading the wrong book. People with great hand-eye coordination, like Rory McIlroy and Dustin Johnson, can pour every ounce of their power into a drive and still hit it reasonably straight. Or with a fade or a draw. But, regardless of which shot shape they utilize, the point is that they can hit a ball really hard, but under control. If you're reading this book, you probably don't have the hand-eye coordination of Dustin Johnson.

So, let's take a look at several techniques that can help you drive your ball consistently under control.

First, it is essential to reinforce a point that is made in every instructional golf book and video. If the goal of this book is not to regurgitate universal techniques for golf, but rather to provide you with specific techniques that can augment your lack of hand-eye coordination, why do I begin the section on hitting the driver with a universal technique? Because so many high-handicap golfers just don't seem to get it.

The universal technique of driving is that the driver is the only club in your bag that you use for hitting the ball on an upswing. With your irons, the best shots are achieved by hitting the ball with a descending blow. With the fairway metals, some golfers, such as Lee Trevino, utilize a descending swing. But most modern-day pros hit the fairway metals with a neutral sweeping shot. But the driver is definitely hit after the clubface has bottomed out and is beginning to ascend.

That seems simple enough. So, why do I say that most high-handicap golfers don't get it. Because we see them teeing up the ball in the middle of their stance. That's the point where the clubface is bottoming out. So, they can't be hitting the ball when the club is ascending. We also see them, even if they have teed up the ball off their front foot, hitting the ball with a short, abbreviated backswing. Instead of taking a wide arc with the driver, they hit down on the ball with a descending blow just like they are supposed to hit their iron shots.

There are several reasons why you want to hit your driver with a wide arc and an ascending blow. First, hitting the ball with a high ball flight is going to generate more distance than that of a low-ball flight. Because the clubface of the driver has significantly less loft, generally nine to twelve degrees, you do not have the loft of the iron that naturally causes the ball to ascend after making contact with a descending clubface. The objective is to let the driver sweep over the ground behind the ball and make contact as the clubface begins to ascend. If you don't hit the ball with an ascending shot that creates loft, then the flight of the ball is going to be low. Hey, like all of us, I have hit some of my longest drives after killing a few gophers in the fairway. But that's not a consistent shot that you can count on to go the farthest with every shot.

Before I hit a drive, I envision the clubface sweeping across the ground and hitting the ball as it rises back up to launch the ball out like a cannon shot. Think about it. If you want to shoot a cannonball as far as possible, do you shoot the cannon at ground level, or do you raise the barrel up and shoot the cannonball high into the sky? Of course, you elevate the cannon. Elevating the flight path of your drive by hitting it with an ascending blow will achieve the same gain in distance.

Secondly, your power is generated by taking a wide arc with the club and building club head speed during the downswing. A brief trip down memory lane will illustrate this principle the best. If you look at golf pros prior to the 1970s, they weren't tall. All the greatest golfers, including Bobby Jones, Ben Hogan, Arnold Palmer, Jack Nicklaus, Gary Player, and Lee Trevino were less than six feet tall. In fact, being tall was considered as a negative for a good golfer. But in the 1980s and 1990s, golfers began to harness the power of a wide arc in generating prodigious drives. And the taller the golfer, the wider the arc. Today, if you go down the list of the top golfers, almost every one of them is over six feet tall. Regardless of how tall you are, you still want to maximize the width of your swing arc and, very importantly, the distance of your swing arc.

In an effective golf shot, the clubhead swings as far away from the body as possible and accelerates as it moves through the downswing. Forget physics. Common sense will tell you that, if the clubhead is accelerating, the extra few inches from the point at the bottom of the swing to a point where the club is ascending, approximately six inches farther in front, results in the clubface contacting the ball with more force.

So, technique number one is to remember that you want to hit your drive with a wide arc and an ascending blow. Obviously, you want to tee up the ball off of your front foot.

In addition, you want to tee the ball higher on the tee. Have you ever looked at the height of golf tees from back in the 1960s? Nowadays, we use those tees for hitting irons off the tee! Today's tees resemble railroad spikes. There's a good reason for that. Utilize the taller tees to tee up your ball at least one-half inch higher than the top of your driver clubhead as it rests on the ground behind the ball. Then, develop a mental image of your clubhead contacting the ball on an ascending blow, just like being fired out of a cannon.

Try taking a K-shaped stance with your body leaning back on your drive. This will encourage the club to hit the ball with an ascending swing. But if it causes you to lose control, go back to a neutral set up with your weight evenly on both legs.

If you read the instructional books, they will encourage you to have a K-shaped stance for your drive. What this means is that your body leans slightly back away from the hole as you assume your stance. If you can pull this off, do it. It will position your body better behind the ball and encourage hitting the ball with an ascending path. But many high-handicap golfers struggle when they lean back in their driving stance. The problem it creates is that it moves your center of gravity behind the ball. For professional golfers, this is what you want, because remember, the professional golfer is bottoming out their swing about six inches behind the ball. But for the amateur, it can encourage them to stub the ground six inches behind the ball. If you are unable to adopt this K-shaped swing, so be it. Set up for your drive in a neutral stance with an equal amount of weight on each foot.

Next, let's explore how to create the widest arc for your shot. If you read the golf instructional books and magazine articles, they will talk about the one-piece takeaway. If your eyes glaze over as you read these articles, don't worry about it. Let's just make it as simple as possible. To initiate the drive, allow your hands to move first before the rest of your body. Have a mental image of extending your arms out as far from your body as possible. Then swing your hands back and into a natural arc around your body. But don't worry about at what point your hips and the rest of your body begin to rotate. If you do, you'll drive yourself crazy. And you'll be thinking about that, rather than focusing on making solid contact with the ball. Simply allow your hips and legs to begin to rotate as soon as it naturally wants to happen.

Some golfers find that a smooth takeaway is easier to initiate if you have some sort of physical motion. Jack Nicklaus was famous for rotating his face to the right before beginning his swing. Other golfers, such as Gary Player, advocate kicking the rear knee toward the ball prior to initiating the swing. Other golfers allow the body to do a forward press before initiating the backswing.

There are both mental and physical benefits to a technique to initiate the backswing. For Jack Nicklaus, it was primarily a mental technique. I'm not sure what benefit turning your face to the right gives you. But psychologically, Jack would tell you that that motion indicated to the body that it was ready to swing the club with confidence.

But there can be physical benefits to a technique to initiate the backswing. The forward press of the body is one such technique. Think about it this way. If you had a bucket of water that was filled all the way to the brim and you wanted to swing the bucket back and through without losing any water, how would you do it? Very few people would start the bucket from a dead standstill. This would tend to cause the water to slosh out of the bucket as it went from motionless to motion. So, most people would slowly swing the bucket slightly forward and then gradually take it back in the other direction. That's the physical benefit of the forward press.

Here's another way to think of it. Why do golfers even do a backswing? If most backswings are hurting the swing by being out of position at the top or causing loss of control as golfers swing too rapidly, why wouldn't you simply take the club up to the top and stop? It would enable you to ensure that the club is in the right position. It would also prevent you from moving from the backswing to the downswing too rapidly.

Trust me, many frustrated and desperate golfers have tried this technique. Maybe for some it helps, but for most people, it's a recipe for disaster. If it worked, you would see really good golfers doing it. But you don't. Why doesn't it work? It's physics. Even if stopping your backswing at the top enables you to be in the right position, when you quickly accelerate the club from a standing position, the rapid acceleration of the club is extremely difficult to control. Like our water bucket analogy, a smooth backswing to the top, followed by a smooth transition to the downswing creates a golf swing with the greatest accuracy and chance of making solid contact with the ball. So, next time you're on the range, try several techniques to initiate your golf swing, such as the forward press.

The next thing to think about during your backswing is to keep your trailing arm as closely anchored to your body as possible. We've covered this technique in several other places in this book, such as in the section on hitting wedges. We've also covered the best technique for doing this, which is the towel drill. Even golfers with the best swings in the business continued to practice with a towel or golf glove under their armpit. Not only do they put it under the armpit of their trailing arm, but they also use the technique for their front arm.

If you allow your trailing elbow to move away from your body, physics dictates that the clubface has moved outside of a good swing plane. Most likely, your club is in more of an upright position (more wrapped around your head than wrapped around your back) at the top of your backswing. This is called casting. That's the motion that you want to use in casting a fly rod. It's not the position you want to have for hitting a golf ball. If your swing is very upright, then when you swing back down into the ball, you are swinging across the back of the ball. This imparts side swing to the ball, generally resulting in a slice. You want your arms to remain close to your body so that the club naturally swings around your body, stays on plane, and makes direct solid contact with the back of the ball.

The subject of swinging on plane needs a little bit more elaboration. The swing plane is simply the direction that the club moves around the body. Let's revisit the most graphic visualization of the swing plane which was in the famous instructional book by Ben Hogan. He used the visual of a plane of glass. The front edge of the plane of glass would be at the back of the ball. The plane of glass would then proceed up and through the golfer's body and culminate above their head. The perfect swing would have the arms and the club, which is simply an extension of the outstretched arms, swinging around the body and up to the top.

In other words, the swing plane is a line that is drawn from the ball up through the shaft of the golf club as the golfer sets up to the ball up through the golfer and above the golfer's back. In a perfect swing, the hands and the golf club are exactly at the other end of that line. A better visual might be two planes of glass. In order to remain on plane, we need to swing between these two planes of glass. If the club was too steep, it would shatter the top plane of glass. If the swing was too shallow and dipped below the swing plane at the top, it would shatter the bottom plane of glass.

What do you need to think about? Simply, keep things simple. As you bring the club back in your downswing, try to maintain the same angle of the club as it moves in an arc around the body. Take the club up to the top. Freeze. You might need for someone to take a picture of you from behind the ball. If you are on plane, you should be able to draw a straight line from the clubhead, down through your arms that

*If you can draw a straight line from the clubhead down through
the shaft and ending at the ball, then your swing is on plane.
That way, you won't be breaking any glass panes!*

points directly to the back of the ball. If your club is too far above your head, you will need to flatten your spine plane. Think about keeping your rear elbow close to your body. If your elbow doesn't fly out, it's hard to have an upright swing. If your swing plane is too shallow (your line comes out somewhere over the ball), then try to swing more up and down, and not so much around the body.

As you swing the club around your body, your club should be able to line up directly with the back of the ball. However, at the top of the backswing, you are no longer able to draw a line down the shaft of the club through the arms and to the back of the ball. Why? Because at the top of the backswing, your wrists have hinged, enabling the club to swing into what is known as a parallel position. If you remember your high school geometry, parallel means two lines that are running side by side and equidistant like the rails of a railroad track. Some golfers can take the club at the top beyond parallel with the head pointing at the ground. John Daly was one of the first modern golfers to break this rule and utilize the additional leverage of the clubface to create more power. But, for the rest of us mortals, the optimal position for the club at the top of the backswing is with the wrists hinged, with the club parallel to the ground, pointed directly to the target. Again, you'll probably need a mirror or a video to see where your club is at the top.

At the top of your backswing, the club should not go any farther than parallel with the ground. If you can go beyond parallel, it's a good source of power. But for most of us, it leads to a loss of control. Also, make sure that your club is pointing towards the target.

We need to look at one other thing when your club gets to the top. This concerns what happens to the wrist of your lead arm. I am going to refer to just what is happening to the wrist of your lead arm, as, at the top, the wrist of your trailing arm will be just the opposite of your lead arm wrist.

At the top, your wrist can be in one of three positions. First, your wrist can be cupped. This means that the wrist of the lead arm is bent so that at the top it is pointing more in the direction that the golfer is facing. The fingers on the lead arm hand are bent so that they are closer to the front of the arm. One way to remember this is that the bend in the hands and arms forms more of the shape of a drinking cup. The second position is called the bowed wrist. Here, your hands bend away from the direction that the golfer is facing. The wrist is bent

It's best to keep your wrist flat at the top. You can experiment with a cupped or bowed wrist. But, for now, let's keep it simple.

so that the fingers are now closer to the back or underside of the arm. The third position is to keep the wrists straight at the top. If you drew a line down the arm, it would extend straight through the wrist and out through the end of the fingers.

Many pros famously bow or cup their wrists at the top of their backswing. This enables them to either draw or fade their drives. Once you get really good, I would suggest you read up on the merits and effects of these techniques and potentially adopt a bent wrist. But for now, let's stick to the basics. Bending your wrists at the top enables golfers to curve the ball one way or the other. The pros can control this. You probably can't. Bending the wrists can lead to erratic shots.

So, for now, just stick to a straight wrist. One good technique is to place a ruler that runs from under your watch, or

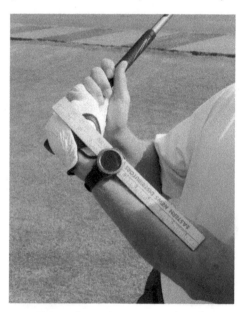

*Inserting a ruler under your watch is a great way
to tell if your wrist is bowing or cupping.*

a similar device, down through the glove on your trail hand. If you try to cup your hands, the ruler prevents it. It will get painful! If you try to bow your wrist, you will be able to feel the back of your hand separating from the ruler. It's a quick way to tell if you are cupping or bending your wrists. You can't wear the ruler when you are out on the course. But use the drill to ingrain the feeling of a straight wrist at the top of your swing.

Our final step in swinging the club may or may not work for you. I'll throw it out there. Give it a try. If it works, it works. If not, you have still gained a few techniques that will help you make solid contact with the ball and improve the quality of your drives.

Where are the most powerful muscles of your body located? If you paid better attention in your anatomy class, you would know that those are the muscles in your upper legs and rear end. So, if you are hitting the club with the most power and where you want to get the greatest distance, doesn't it make sense that you want to tap into these powerful muscles? But most high-handicap golfers don't do it. Instead, they use only the weaker muscles in their arms as they take an arms-only swing.

Why do they do this? There are primarily two reasons. First, they don't know that you can use your hips and legs to hit the ball. Let me illustrate. Hand a plastic baseball bat to a five-year-old. Ask them to swing at an imaginary ball. They will do an arms-only swing. They don't know that to hit a powerful swing, you need to incorporate your hips. It's not intuitive. A golf swing looks like it should be done with just the arms. But now you know.

Secondly, most high-handicap golfers struggle to make contact with the ball by just making a simple arms-only swing. Now, mixing in the movement of the hips adds another element of complexity. And it's one more thing that can go wrong. So, as I said above, try to incorporate the hips and legs into the swing. If it doesn't work, it doesn't work. Stick with the arms only and hit from the tees that are closest to the pin!

One other thing to notice. While I have mentioned with other clubs, primarily the long irons and the fairway metals, that you want to incorporate firing with your hips if you can pull it off, I haven't really dwelt very much on this technique. Why am I dwelling on it now? Because the driver offers you the most margin for error. It offers the widest hitting surface of any of the clubs. The modern drivers are designed with a curving face so that, even if you hit the ball a bit off of the sweet spot, the physics of the clubface allows many of your "close" shots to recover. It won't get you into any long drive competitions, but it will help to correct your mishit and keep you out of the woods. So, I would suggest that you try firing the hips with the driver where you have the greatest chance of pulling it off. It if works, try it with the other clubs. If it doesn't, at least incorporate it into your driver shot.

So, how does this hip and leg thing work? When you have swung the driver around your body, on plane, parallel to the ground at the top and pointing down the line toward the target, pause. Yes, it's the familiar pause. As discussed earlier, it will be more of a mental pause than a physical pause. But think pause, nonetheless. The pause with the driver is actually more important than the mental pause with the other clubs. With the other clubs, the pause is there to make sure you have taken a full swing and that you aren't rushing the downswing.

With the driver, it actually gives you a chance to switch body parts.

Once you arrive at the top with a backswing that has been totally arms-oriented, you now initiate a movement from your lower body. How does it work? Well, different golfers describe it in a wide variety of ways. For me, I am pressing forward with my hips. Other golfers say that they are feeling the thrust more in their upper legs or even their knees. Very importantly, it isn't a sway. Many golfers, who are first learning to fire their hips, simply sway forward with the hips. Instead, it's more of a swivel. Think about it. What are your hips doing in the backswing? They aren't swaying backward. That would be the sway that moves your center of gravity back behind the ball, leading to the dreaded clunk into the dirt shot. Instead, you want your hips to stay reasonably centered, but to turn around (remember the hinge of the door?) and rotate backward.

A lot of analysis has been done on the most effective position in the backswing. I won't dwell a lot on the technical stuff. But suffice it to say that the hips generally rotate about half of the distance of the shoulders. Your shoulders should rotate at approximately a 90° angle, whereas your hips should rotate, at most, at a 45° angle. Why do we say at most? Wouldn't the farther you wind up your hips be better for generating distance? No. Remember, the objective of a great drive is to generate potential energy, called kinetic energy. Think of a rubber band. When you wind up a rubber band, it creates stored power. When you let the rubber band go, that power is unleashed. The farther back you stretch the rubber band in a slingshot, the farther the projectile goes. So, at the top of your backswing, you want to feel the sensation that your hips are taut and ready to explode in a burst of power. It's the dynamic tension between the distance that the hips are wound and the greater distance that the shoulders are wound that generates power.

Therefore, firing the hips isn't swaying the body back toward the front with the hips leading the way. Firing the hips is proactively unwinding the hips. If you swung back down with just the hands, the hips would eventually unwind. If not, you would walk around funny for the rest of your life. But it would be reactive unwinding of the hips. You want it to be proactive. That means you initiate the downswing by actively unwinding the hips.

Does this mean that you have to add a swing thought to your swing? Unfortunately, the answer is probably yes. Athletically gifted folks are able to naturally wind up their body and initiate firing their hips without really thinking about it. But for the rest of us, it doesn't come so naturally. Even after learning to fire my hips decades ago, I still have to think about it in order to initiate the move. So, I try to hit my drives with only two swing thoughts. I have one thought as I begin my backswing. It's usually something like, "low and slow." But if I am working on something like keeping my wrists from bowing or cupping, I might use that swing thought. But that's it. I have just one thought as I begin my backswing.

Then, once I reach the pause at the top, my one thought is "fire those hips." I try to keep it as simple as possible. Even so, it's one of the hardest things in golf. Have you ever watched a professional golf tournament and seen one of the guys who does this for money yank their tee shot over two fairways? When they show it in slow motion, it wasn't their stance or grip. It wasn't that their takeaway was incorrect. No. It is usually that they either fired their hips too early or too late. So, if the pros struggle with it, where does that leave the rest of us?

For a pro, firing their hips means that they are swinging the club with enough force to drive it three hundred yards. If we are lucky, we clear two hundred yards. The overall speed of our swing is slower. But there is a bit of consolation of us hitting the ball a lot slower. First, it helps to get the right rhythm when the overall swing is slower. It's also easier to square up the clubface. I've now run out of benefits of a slow golf swing! But it's kind of like saying that short people bump their heads less often. Take advantage of the hand you have been dealt. Take advantage of your slower swing speed to add firing your hips to your driver swing. As I said, give it a try. If it works, it will add significant distance to your drives. If you add the firing of the hips and that extra move totally kills your ability to make solid contact with your driver, then remove it from your swing portfolio. Go back to the maximum force swing that you can control.

PUTTING

We have arrived at the area of the game where a more mechanical approach to the game will have the greatest positive impact on your score. How many three putts do you take per round? If you don't know, you should. It's relatively easy to track. After every hole, write down the number of putts that you took in the lower right-hand corner of that hole on the scorecard. After the round, it's easy to tally up the number.

So, let me ask the question again, how many three putts do you average in a round of golf? Two? Five? Ten? If your average score is over one hundred, you probably have at least ten three putts per round. If you average in the nineties, you probably have at least three or four three putts per round. But, in addition to those deadly three putts, you probably had at least four or five holes where your two putt from five feet could have easily been a one putt. In total, if you are able to reduce your number of excess putts by at least ten putts, your score of ninety-five just became an eighty-five! And that's not factoring in any improvement in your driving, iron play, wedge play, or bunker shots. So, you can quickly see the importance of improving your putting.

There's good news. One of the most demonstrable improvements to your game of utilizing a more mechanical approach will come in your putting. As you know, the theme of this book is to not dwell upon the universal teachings of a shot, but merely to introduce more dependable user-friendly techniques for those golfers with poor hand-eye coordination. But I must caution you. This chapter contains the most advice for throwing out the traditional instruction and replacing it with mechanical solutions. But we have to do what we have to do.

Before we get to the actual mechanical putting technique, it is essential to explore a little bit of universal instruction. I'm referring to your mental approach to a putt. The best book on putting I ever read is *Putting Out of Your Mind* by Dr. Bob Rotella. You will notice that the word putting has two different usages. Putting can refer to the golf stroke that you make on the green. But that's also the spelling of the word putting, as in placing something somewhere. So, in this book, which by the way is my favorite title for a golf book, Bob Rotella has tempted us with the prospect of hitting the best putts of our life. But he is also giving us the method for doing this, which is clearing our mind in order to have the best technique.

In his book, Bob Rotella tells us that most putts are missed not through our physical technique, but through our mental process. How often do you stand over a six-foot putt with absolutely no confidence that you are going to make the putt? If you're reading this book, it's probably quite often.

So, what's the solution? Bob Rotella tells us to begin by sizing up the putt. First, how far away is the ball from the hole? As a reformed feel golfer and newly minted mechanical golfer, don't feel embarrassed about pacing off your putt. Your playing partners might look at you kind of funny. They might be tempted to assess you a penalty for slow play. But, when you start sinking more and more of those twenty-foot putts, they're going to have a newfound appreciation of the Pacing Putter.

Next, determine if your putt is uphill or downhill. A quick trip to the side of the putt should determine this. But also, don't forget the value of gaining early intelligence. One of the best places to view the green is from about twenty to thirty yards away. As you are walking or driving to the green, look at the green to gain a quick impression of whether you have an uphill or downhill putt.

The same thing applies to the break of the putt. Will it break to the left or the right? Is it a small break, or a major break? The best advice I have ever read is to imagine that if you poured a bucket of water on the green, where would it flow? Wherever the water would flow, that is where your ball is going to go.

Another technique is to look at the color of the grass. Shiny grass means that the grain is moving away from you. Darker grass means that it is growing toward you. This difference in color can be subtle. It's best seen when contrasting the color. From behind the ball, look at the grass in the line of your putt. Form a mental image of the sheen of the grass. Then rotate around and look back away from your putt. Mentally compare the two. Did the grass between your ball and the hole look shinier or duller than the grass behind your ball? That should provide valuable intelligence.

If you are able to plumb bob, my hat is off to you. I've read instructional book after instructional book, and I have still not mastered this technique. But, if you are able to add this to your green reading technique, more power to you.

Once you've collected all of this intelligence and determined where you want to hit the ball and how hard you want to hit it, then completely put this analysis out of your mind. The objective of your pre-putt routine is to give your putt the best chance of going in the hole. Another great sport psychologist put it a bit differently. Dick Coop once said, "You can't make a putt. You can only make a stroke."

So, once your decision making is completed, wipe your brain clean. Sure, something can happen to your putt. You could have totally misread it. There could be a small pebble in the way that kicks your ball off-line. But more putts are missed because the golfer is still thinking while over the putt.

Not only are they thinking about the putt, but the more they think, the more likely they are to second-guess and doubt that the ball is going to go into the hole. Fretting about that pebble in your line isn't going to make the pebble go away. If it knocks your ball off-line, so be it. But, don't let your thought process cause you to miss more putts. Once you have analyzed the shot and decided exactly what putt you're going to hit, let your mind go blank. Just hit the ball.

Once you get to the point where you are simply executing the predetermined shot, more putts are going to go in the hole. This is going to have a dramatic positive effect on your confidence. There are other good techniques for putting, such as putting to a spot other than the hole so that the ball naturally breaks toward the hole. Or using a pre-alignment spot, such as a discoloration of the grass to line up your putt. These are techniques that you'll find in every instructional book or video, so I won't comment further on these techniques.

But, now let's get to the secret weapon. Let's discuss how a more mechanical approach to putting works. This technique starts with the assumption that you are most likely not a feel putter. Just because you suffer from less-than-optimal hand-eye coordination and struggle to make solid contact with your irons, fairway metals, and driver does not mean that you can't be a feel putter. If you are able to stand over a twenty-five-foot putt and instinctively bring the putter back and through with a stroke that sends the ball up to the edge of the cup, don't change a thing. Also, remind me not to take you on in a free throw shooting competition.

But, if you struggle to determine the right stroke to use to send the putt the proper distance, read on. Let me illustrate what I mean by the difference between a feel putter and a mechanical putter. When I took a series of lessons with the club pro, we ultimately ended up on the practice green. Before hitting a twenty-five-foot putt, the pro could see that I was making some sort of mental calculation. In other words, I was utilizing the technique that I'm about to describe to you, which I had stumbled onto years earlier. Despite the fact that I rolled the ball up to the edge of the cup, he said, "What are you doing? Why is your head nodding?"

I proceeded to describe to him the technique that I was using. He simply looked at me with a puzzled stare. He said, "There's no reason to do all of that. It's just distracting you from making a good putt. Simply size up the distance to the cup, other factors such as whether the putt is uphill or downhill, the direction of the break, and then just hit the ball. It's just like shooting free throws. Or tossing a piece of trash into the wastebasket. Just let your natural sense of distance kick in."

Using his technique, I proceeded to hit the next putt fifteen feet beyond the cup. After compensating, I hit the next putt halfway to the hole. After a few more futile efforts, the pro threw up his arms and said, "Okay, go back to your technique."

So, what is this technique that can be used by the distance-challenged putter to roll the ball up to the hole every time? I call it the dollar bill/ruler technique. It is predicated on physics. It's the putting version of Iron Byron. Think of it this way. If you are on a flat surface with the grass at a constant level of density and break, if you pull the putter face back one inch and strike the ball, your ball will go basically the same distance every time. It's just physics.

Therefore, the first thing that you need to do is to create a technique whereby you are able to gauge how far back you are pulling the head of the putter. The first visual image I use is a dollar bill. A dollar bill is approximately six inches long. As you stand behind the ball, visualize a dollar bill lying behind the ball. If you pulled the putter face back to the edge of the dollar bill, you have pulled the putter blade back six inches.

Don't lay down a dollar bill when putting in a game. Your partner will think you are paying up early. But lay down a dollar bill when practicing. Memorize that image and you can gauge the distance of your backswing for putts up to six inches.

Halfway back is three inches. One-third of the way back is two inches. Using this visual tool, you are able to pull back the face of the putter to a common distance within six inches each time.

For a longer putt, you now want to visualize a ruler. Pull out the old grade school ruler. As you know, it's exactly twelve inches. Lay it down behind the ball. You're using the visual of the dollar bill up to six inches. So, with the ruler, you only have to worry about the distance between inches six and twelve. Go somewhere where nobody can see you and work on this technique. Lay down the ruler. Ingrain the distance in your brain. Then utilize this technique to pull back the face of the putter to a common distance each time.

If your putt is longer than twelve inches, you are going to have to use a little imagination. For an eighteen-inch putt, pull the face of the putter back twelve inches, or the distance of the ruler. Stop there. Then imagine that you are bringing the putter face back another six inches, or the length of the dollar

Use a ruler to ingrain the mental image of putts up to twelve inches.

bill. For a putt with a backswing of twenty-four inches, you would pull back the clubface the length of one ruler, stop, and the length of a second ruler. Get it?

Next, we have to figure out how far your putt goes based on each inch of backswing. You can only do this through practice. Head out to the practice green. Lay down your dollar bill. Slowly pull the face of the putter back one-sixth of the dollar bill or one inch. If you are struggling to figure out how far back one-sixth of the dollar bill is, then lay down the ruler. There you can see exactly how far back one inch is.

Now, smoothly swing the face of the putter back one inch and then with the same pace and tempo, swing the clubface back through the ball. In feel putting, the pros will advise you that your swing through the ball should be roughly the same length as your backswing. But that's not going to work in our technique, which the pros and the announcers label as a "pop" putt. Why? Because you'll see that the same distance you swing the clubface back two inches, the feel putter will pull back six inches. How can your putt, with a two-inch backswing, go the same distance as the pro's putt with a six-inch backswing? Because he only swings through six inches beyond the ball. With the pop putting technique, you generate more speed because you swing through the ball farther than two inches.

How far? Your follow-through will take your putter head as far out in front as your smooth, steady, and rhythmical swing takes it. You want a natural, unforced swing of the putter. So, you don't really care how far your putter blade goes after the club is no longer connected with the back of the ball. It's a moot point. The important thing for a mechanical putt is how much force the putter applies to the back of the ball when it makes contact with the ball.

But you might ask, don't all of the pros say that your putter should go back and past the ball the same distance for a real good reason? Yes, if you putt the way they do. Remember, they are putting by feel. In a feel putt, you are mentally determining the amount of force you want to apply to the back of the ball to achieve the distance you want the ball to go. Golfers who putt by feel are going to bring the putter back much farther than you will using the mechanical method. If they pull the putter back twice or three times as far back as you do, but then apply enough forward motion to carry the putter way out in front of them, they will hit the putt way too hard. Think of their shortened follow-through as simply a "governor" that controls the force that they apply to the ball.

A smooth, rhythmical putting stroke with the putter head going the same distance it goes after making contact as the distance it went on the backswing works great for the feel putter. After they mentally calculate the amount of force to apply to make the ball go the required distance, they pull back the putter face by the length that their brain tells them to pull it back. You can easily prove this. After a feel putter strokes a twenty-foot putt, ask them, "How far did you pull back the putter blade?" They will look at you like you are crazy. They will say, "How should I know? I have no idea. I pulled it back as far as I needed to hit the ball the distance I wanted to hit it."

And that must be really nice to be able to do that. But, if you struggle with distance control like I and most high-handicap golfers do, you just don't have the sense of feel to allow your brain to determine the distance you pull back (and follow through on the other side of the ball) during the putt. So, you have to use a system in which you definitely know how far back you pull the putter head. And in order to hit the ball the same distance when you pull back the putter head two inches and the feel putter pulls it back six inches, you have to allow the putter head to swing through farther than just two inches on the other side of the ball. You do this by allowing the putter blade to flow farther out than the distance of your backswing. You allow it to flow out as far as the natural momentum of the putt carries it.

But you might ask, aren't we told that we should have a good follow-though and not to "quit" on a shot? That the smooth follow-through is what carries the ball the distance we need a shot to go? Yes, that's true of a longer shot, such as a chip shot. If you quit on the follow-through, your chip shot is going to fall far short of the pin. So, if a long follow-through gives us the longer distance we need on a wedge shot, why wouldn't a longer follow-through cause the putt to go too far?

Well, let's go back to the physics. In the chip shot, does the ball stay on the face of the wedge all of the way through the follow-through? Of course not. It stays on the blade for a fraction of a second before rocketing out into the air. So, if the ball leaves the clubface almost immediately after making contact with the blade, why would a six-inch follow-through not be the same as a twenty-six-inch follow-through? Because the length of the follow-through is actually a by-product of the amount of force in your downswing. In other words, if you hit a chip with only a six-inch follow-through, then the amount of force with which you made contact with the ball is less than the amount of force that generates a twenty-six-inch follow-through!

So, let's apply that to the mechanical putt. Allowing the putter head to carry through to a lengthy follow-through doesn't cause the putt to go too far. Remember, the ball is only on the putter face for a fraction of a second. But the force necessary to generate a lengthy follow-through is the amount of force necessary for your controlled, measured two-inch backswing to go the same length as the six-inch backswing done by the feel putter. Make sense? So, head to the practice green and practice putts with a backswing of two, three, four, five, and more inches. But always swing the putter face through with the same tempo. Allow the distance that the putter is pulled back to determine the amount of force applied to the back of the ball.

Now that we know to allow our follow-through to be naturally determined by the amount of force generated by a smooth, rhythmical putt, we can get back to our measurements. Hit the putt with a one-inch backswing. Note how far the ball goes. For me, a one-inch backswing with a smooth, rhythmical forward swing rolls the ball about five feet. It will vary by person. A smooth swing by a stronger golfer might carry the ball forward about six feet. A weaker putter might hit it only four feet. But the secret is to swing with the same rhythm each time. Just because you lack the feel of a great golfer doesn't mean that, with constant practice, you can't achieve the same rhythmical stroke every time you hit a putt.

Now, bring the putter head back two inches. How far does the putt go? For me, it will be about ten feet. Next, bring it back half of the dollar bill image or three inches. If you are hitting it with a consistent rhythm, the three-inch backswing should cause the ball to go about three times the length it went when you pulled back the putter head one inch. A five-inch backswing should cause the ball to go about five times as far.

So, here comes the part that drives the pros crazy. When you step behind the ball, count off the distance to the flag, using the average length of your one-inch putt. You would visualize the first five feet (or however far you hit a one-inch backswing) and count to one. Then visualize the next five feet and count to two. Continue to add an inch for every five-foot distance that you visualize in your mind.

If the distance to the flag is about five feet, you count to one. You literarily are counting in your head. That's what the pro thought was so strange about my pre-shot routine. He could literally see me nodding my head as I counted off each five-foot length. If you, like me, hit your putt five feet with a one-inch backswing, for a fifteen-foot putt, you will count to three. You know to pull back the putter face three inches.

Take your stance as if you were addressing the putt, but about six inches back from the ball. Allow enough space to take your practice swing without having any risk of accidently hitting your ball. Take a practice swing. Feel the putter blade go back three inches (or half of that mental image of the dollar bill). Then swing through the putt. Ingrain that tempo in your muscle memory. Now, confidently step up to the ball. We are going to take a second practice putt. But the second practice stroke is taken with your putter face behind the ball. So, we only pull it back to establish the muscle memory of the length that we pull back the putt. Slowly bring the putter face back behind the ball. You are now ready to putt.

Why two practice swings? They each have a different objective. The practice putt made to the side of the ball is to ingrain the speed and tempo of the putt. That is where you ingrain in your brain that you are hitting a nice, leisurely putt using the same tempo on every putt. The practice putt made once you have addressed the ball is to ingrain in your muscle memory how far back you pull the putter head. Think of this practice putt as the waggle for your putt.

Now, pull the putter back three inches and stroke the putter through the ball. Don't look at your putter blade going back! People with poor hand-eye coordination are perfectly capable of whiffing a putt. Believe me, I've done it many a time. Well, maybe not totally whiffing the ball, but hitting it on the toe, on the heel, or anywhere other than the sweet spot of the putter face. For us to make solid contact with the ball on a putt, we have to place our total focus on the back of the ball and making solid contact at that point. That's why the final practice putt is so important. You have to ingrain the length of your backswing in your muscle memory because you can't look at the putter face going back. Feel how far back you need to take the putter (using your dollar bill or ruler imagery), focus on the back of the ball, and then allow your muscle memory to duplicate that practice swing. I know it sounds hard. But, with a bit of practice, you can pull it off. I did it. You can too.

One word of caution about this technique. Just like with any other shot, the high-handicap golfer tends to speed up their putt in order to get it over with as soon as possible. You have heard of the yips, I'm sure. The primary thing involved with the yips is an involuntary jerk of the hands and arms that causes you to speed up the putt, which usually results in pulling or pushing the putt. You do not have to have the yips to simply rush the putt because you want to get it over with.

You must fight this urge to speed up the putt. The best technique to do this is to allow a brief pause at the end of your backswing. The pause has to be brief. You want your putt to be a natural flowing motion. If you pull back the putter face and pause for more than a very brief amount of time, then in order to initiate your swing back through the ball, you have to apply more force than you would like. Remember the analogy with swinging the bucket of water? You do not want your putter face to come to a lengthy halt that can only be followed by a forward push with your hands. This applied forward force tends to take your putter face off-line. You're going to find that you're going to come across the ball. That's going to lead you to push or pull your putt. So, make sure your pause is brief.

In fact, what you are going to find is, if you look at your putt on video, you probably won't even see the putter face pause at all. In other words, the pause is really more of the mental pause that we discussed earlier. Instead of bringing the putter face back and immediately initiating the forward swing, mentally allow the putter face to come back, pause, and rhythmically swing through the ball. Again, this is one technique that you simply need to practice, practice, practice.

There is one more benefit of the dollar bill/ruler visualization technique. Feel putters are told to not bring the putter face straight back and through. They are taught to allow the putter head to open and close in a natural fashion as they bring the putter face back and the arms rotate around the solid core of the body. Amazingly, good feel putters are able to allow the putter face to open and close and come back on an inside track and then magically come back perfectly perpendicular to the ball at contact. But the rest of us can't do that!

Our mechanical technique does call for us to pull the putter face straight back and straight through. How do we do that? Well, the dollar bill/ruler techniques aid us in doing this. In our visualization, we are pulling the club back over the dollar bill or the ruler. In other words, if we are pulling the putter head back twelve inches, we visualize pulling the putter head straight back from the start to the finish of our imaginary ruler. Using this visualization technique not only helps us to visualize the distance we pull back the putt, but also to visualize pulling the putter face straight back and straight through.

Once you have this technique down pat, you might get a few quizzical comments from your playing partners. They might make fun of your pop putting technique. But here are a couple of things to remember. First, from the early days of golf through the 1960s, the most common putting technique was the pop technique. Why? The consistency of the greens was not what it is today. Knowing this, the early golfers had to rely on a technique that delivered a more consistent length, regardless of the consistency of the putting surface. Nowadays, with consistent putting surfaces, feel putters can be confident using their intuitive distance control. But again, you don't have that same intuitive feel. So, you need to go back and utilize the same pop technique used so well by the early successful golfers. But, if this is a technique used successfully by Old Tom Morris, then why can't you use it successfully today? I would say that this putting technique has a pretty good pedigree.

Secondly, many pros continue to use this technique today. One of the most successful pop putters is Brandt Snedeker. And Sneds is considered to be one of the best putters around. I'm guessing that Brandt Snedeker has a pretty good sense of feel. But he still utilizes a pop putting technique because he simply feels more confident that it will deliver the results that he wants on each and every putt.

Another great putter is Bryson DeChambeau. I recently heard a golf announcer say that DeChambeau also utilizes the technique of bringing the putter face back a consistent measurable distance with each putt. I tried to confirm this with Bryson, but he didn't respond to my calls! But, if you think about it, it makes sense. DeChambeau is one of the most analytical players on the pro tour. After all, he has developed techniques such as having every club the same length and swinging every club in a similar method. It's not surprising that this mechanical approach to managing the distance of your putts would appeal to an analytical mind such as his. So, the next time one of your playing partners pokes fun at your pop putt, just tell them that Snedeker or DeChambeau taught you that technique!

SUMMARY

Charles Dickens once said, "A small key can open a very heavy door." The purpose of this book is to be that small key. Golf is a tough sport. Many wise sports commentators have called it the cruelest game. It's humbling, and often amusing, to watch athletes at the top of the heap in other sports struggle to hit a golf ball. Let's be honest. Some of the spectators who go to a celebrity golf tournament to watch the best athletes in the world shank the ball are the same ones who go to car races to watch all of the wrecks.

It's already been established that if you got through this entire book, then you struggle to make solid contact with the ball. You've taken more golf lessons than you care to admit. Your YouTube history is peppered with one golf instructional video after another. Your collection of golf instructional books resembles the New York Public Library. But nothing seems to have helped. That's because it all comes back to one central point. The people giving those lessons, filming those videos, and writing those books have a skill set that you don't possess. What you need is a way to compensate for this lack of hand-eye coordination. You need techniques that enable you to compensate and to be able to make solid contact with the ball.

Like Darwin's quotation, golf is like a heavy door. It is imposing and scary. But the tiny key can help us overcome it every time. Each tip in this book is like a tiny key. But not every key opens every door. Some of these tips will work and help you out. Others just won't work for you. All I would ask is that you head to the range. Don't try them all at once. Golf needs to become a game of simple. Perhaps, try a different chapter (or type of club) with each outing. If something works for you, do it over and over again. Ingrain it into your mental game and your muscle memory.

If you find enough of these tips and techniques work, you can make a significant improvement in your game. And maybe, just maybe, you'll be able to print out that handicap card with the ever-elusive single-digit handicap!

Larry Carpenter

CPSIA information can be obtained
at www.ICGtesting.com
Printed in the USA
JSHW040350291021
19899JS00001B/1